Don't Say A Word

He told me not to tell, but one day
the hurting had to stop.

Kate Marshall

with Linda Watson-Brown

JOHN BLAKE

Published by John Blake Publishing,
2.25, The Plaza,
535 Kings Road,
Chelsea Harbour,
London SW10 0SZ

www.johnblakebooks.com

www.facebook.com/johnblakebooks 🔲
twitter.com/jblakebooks 🔲

First published in paperback in 2018

PB ISBN: 978 1 78606 926 9
Ebook ISBN: 978 1 78946 023 0

British Library Cataloguing-in-Publication Data:
A catalogue record for this book is available from the British Library.

Design by www.envydesign.co.uk

Printed and bound in Great Britain by Clays Ltd, Elcograf S.p.A.

1 3 5 7 9 10 8 6 4 2

Papers used by John Blake Publishing are natural, recyclable products made
from wood grown in sustainable forests. The manufacturing processes conform
to the environmental regulations of the country of origin.

Every attempt has been made to contact relevant copyright-holders, but some
were unobtainable. We would be grateful if the appropriate people could
contact us.

John Blake Publishing is an imprint of Bonnier Books UK Ltd
www.bonnierbooks.co.uk

Don't Say A Word

This book is dedicated to the five loves of my life – love you all for ever, bibbies – and to anyone past, present and future who feels like they don't matter. You do.

Contents

Prologue

PART ONE

Chapter 1	BEFORE HELL	7
Chapter 2	A DIFFERENT WORLD	23
Chapter 3	GRATEFUL	39
Chapter 4	GROWING PAINS	53
Chapter 5	PRINCESS	69
Chapter 6	FAMILY	85
Chapter 7	OUT	101

PART TWO

| Chapter 8 | THIS IS WHAT YOU ARE | 123 |
| Chapter 9 | JUMP | 137 |

Chapter 10   TRUE COLOURS   149
Chapter 11   TRAPPED   165
Chapter 12   GHOSTS   185

PART THREE

Chapter 13   LOVE   205
Chapter 14   GUILTY   219
Chapter 15   LEE AND BETH   231
Chapter 16   ELLIE   245
Chapter 17   ELLIE'S INQUEST   265

Epilogue   271
Acknowledgements   277

Prologue

I DON'T KNOW why, but that Friday night in April I didn't check my email the way I usually do.

My habit is to sit in the car for a bit, scroll through to see if there is anything I need to deal with, then head inside to my sanctuary, to home, where everything is how I need it to be. You'd think that work in a coroner's office would be peaceful, but the truth is, the demands of the dead are always there, pinching at the edges of life, asking you to pay attention; so, especially at weekends, I need to shed that life before I can move on to my own.

But that night . . . that night . . .

I went inside, made a cup of tea and flopped on the sofa for a bit, then remembered. Email. One eye on the phone, one eye on some rubbish TV programme, I'd give them a quick glance, then delete, try to relax for the weekend. Until— that isn't right.

Someone I used to hear from a lot.

Someone I've had to distance myself from because it isn't helping their recovery process.

Someone who knows that's what we need to do for a bit and who doesn't email.

It's a different address to the one she usually sends messages from and the heading is: *PLEASE READ!!!*

I take a deep breath, say to myself, 'Kate, you'll regret this' and open it.

Did you know that Ellie killed herself last November?

Those words. Those stark, cold words. I had no idea that they would throw me into the past, throw me into reflecting on everything I had been through – and also push me forward to this. To deciding to tell it all.

Ellie, I think, *not Ellie, please, not Ellie.*

The thought that she had gone had an instant effect on me. I saw her face, her laughing beautiful face, and I was propelled back into my own past. Ellie, the troubled, amazing, misunderstood victim of so much.

I thought she'd be a survivor.

I thought she'd be like me.

I had wanted her to get through it all, and to rise. To find love, to find help and to rise like a phoenix. She'd be battered and bruised – all of us survivors were if anyone bothered to look closely enough – but she would rise, she could. Those words changed all of that. *Ellie killed herself last November.* Was it true? Had she really left us?

Shaking, I thought to my past, to my childhood and adulthood, to all that happened and all that had brought me here. It was almost instant. The realisation that I needed to tell it, I needed to tell it all no matter who would be offended. I knew that there would be those who would say 'let sleeping dogs lie.' The past is the past after all – except it isn't. It colours so much of our present, even when we think we have moved on. It's not my job to protect other people any longer, and it's not my job to cater to them at the expense of my truth.

You have a voice. We all have a voice. Don't let anyone tell you when you need to use it, don't feel that you need to speak at any time other than the one that is right for you. But this is my time. This is my voice, these are my words, and I have to speak. Not just for me, but for anyone who has lived any of this, and for the children who are still in the middle of it all . . . and for Ellie, for all the Ellies out there. Here is my story, and here are my reasons for fighting.

PART 1

CHAPTER 1

Before Hell

I HAVE ONE very clear image in my head. In it, my sister and I are standing on our perfectly manicured front lawn. She is wearing a yellow T-shirt with a picture of a strawberry on the front – a T-shirt that would eventually be passed down to me – and I'm wearing a blue denim, knee-length dress. Our hair is immaculately brushed into pigtails with matching ribbons, and I have a plaster on my knee. Our arms are draped round our mother's neck as she kneels on the grass between us, smiling, holding us in an embrace.

That photo is my first real memory of my childhood; I still have it somewhere, which is probably why the recollection remains so vivid in my mind. I don't know the significance of it other than it is a photo that looks so idealistic, so perfect . . . and I want that. I want to believe there were moments in my childhood like that. It was one of the few times in my life that I can recall my mother in what seemed to be a clichéd maternal role while we were all still together: her, me, my sisters and my brothers. I would spend years wanting the kind of mummy she appeared to be in that photo and to have the type of life the picture suggested.

It was taken at our house in Stoke-on-Trent, the place where I was born. We lived in a tiny, predominantly rural, pocket of the town, on a long winding street of houses set back from the road behind a steep grassy bank. They were mainly council properties, as was ours; only a few were privately owned back then. Our four-bedroomed semi-detached council house held my parents – Gloria and Derek – and their seven children, with me being the youngest. When I came along in April 1972, Mum was twenty-eight years old and Dad was thirty-two. The family was already bursting at the seams by the time I turned up, and Mum had been having babies since she was only sixteen. Wendy was twelve, Jill was eleven, Debbie was ten, Peter was nine, Andrew was eight and Michelle was four. I've often wondered if I was a mistake, as there seemed to be a bit of a gap after Michelle and, indeed, a similar gap between her and Andrew, whereas all my other siblings came along at the rate of one a year.

It doesn't take too much imagination to envisage our household as a hectic and boisterous one. Dad worked on the bins and, as far back as I can remember, Mum worked as a barmaid at a local pub. I remember her going to work in the evenings when I was in bed and also on a Sunday lunchtime, when the highlight of the day would be Dad taking me to pick her up. I would be given crisps, chocolate and tomato juice from behind the bar while we were waiting for her to finish and I felt like the queen of everything!

I have very few memories of my mother during this period of my life and don't recall seeing much of her; those memories are mostly made up of the things that my siblings and I would get up to in the evenings when our parents were both at work. The older girls were teenagers by this time and had been given responsibility for looking after the younger ones, and this took the form of them, in the time before bed, blasting out music on the record player while we all sang and danced along. A song that always takes me back to that time is the Nolan Sisters' 'I'm in the Mood for Dancing'. I clearly remember my sister Debbie making up dance routines for me and Michelle, swinging us round to make us dizzy, then dropping us down on the carpet, where we giggled helplessly on the floor. There were posters of David Essex and David Cassidy plastered over the walls of our bedroom, a room that Michelle and I shared with Wendy, then, when Wendy married and moved out, with Debbie.

The images I have of my parents from my childhood

are very clear in my mind. Mum wore a lot of make-up when she went out. She had big brown eyes and dyed her hair dark. She was very attractive and played up those huge eyes of hers, as she'd always had compliments about them. She had a good figure too – although her weight would yo-yo as she got older – and liked to dress in tight-fitting tops, and the flared jeans or trousers of the 1970s. Her self-worth always came from how others saw her, mostly men, and she presented herself in a very sexual way, sticking her chest out, dousing herself in Avon Musk perfume, or Tweed.

It was a crowded house and money was scarce. The rooms were sparsely furnished and there were rarely any luxuries. Our clothes mainly consisted of hand-me-downs, but I remember a lot of fun times and generally feeling loved and safe, probably due to me holding the enviable position of being the baby of such a large family. Food was never an issue to me back then – I was very skinny and probably didn't eat much. I don't remember even thinking much about food really; we would always sit at the table together at mealtimes and 'bagsy' our favourite bits from other people's plates in case they were planning to leave any – which was rare – but I don't recall ever feeling really hungry or it being the issue it was to become in the years ahead.

I have many more memories of my dad throughout this time than I have of Mum. He was a handsome man, with dark hair and weathered skin from his days outside working on the bins. He smelled of Brut or Old Spice or Denim aftershave, and I would sniff it when we hugged – it was a real 'Dad' smell, which still takes me back. I would sit on his lap and marvel at the colour of his muscular arms, which were the shade of strong tea in my childlike eyes, comparing them to my own pale, scrawny ones. He smelled of cut grass, with a big smile on his face and an infectious laugh that poured out of him. Dad was a keen, skilled gardener, and I always remember him spending the summer months tending to our plot, putting little plastic windmills at the front of the house that would spin in the breeze. I used to feel such pride when other people looked over, sure they were admiring our garden and thinking how clever my dad must be. In the huge rear garden, which backed onto open fields, there was a swing that would often lift out of the ground when the fittings came loose. If we swung too high it would screech as if to warn us, and we'd know that Dad would have to come and work his magic on it again.

These are safe memories, long summers when Dad grew gooseberries, rhubarb, potatoes and many more delicious things, when there was a bounty to choose from in our garden, and I would stuff fat handfuls of berries into my mouth while filling a plastic bowl with the remainder if I could bear to part with them. The juice would run down my chin and I'd be in fruit heaven, completely lost in the moment – and safe, so safe. It was to be these memories of spending summer evenings with Dad in the garden while Mum was at work that I'd desperately hold on to for years to come.

Mum wasn't a bad parent at this point, she was just absent really. My memories are of my siblings more than anything, as they were always there. Summers were a cliché of being chucked out in the morning with them, and not coming back until teatime. It was a safe area and it was a safe early time in my life.

As the youngest, I knew that the others were all growing up and doing things that would be a long time coming for me. Pete got a paper round when he was fourteen, so I'd be about five, and it seemed a very adult thing to do. I'd watch him head off, riding his bicycle down the narrow gravel lanes, and beg to go with him. He'd often indulge me, pulling me along behind him on my little plastic go-kart tied to his bike with string. I would love pedalling along in that way, my skinny little legs going nineteen to the dozen, then jumping off and following him up path after path to push the papers through the letterboxes. It must have taken him three times longer than it should have done with me 'helping'. I hold memories like these so precious in my heart, and they make me reflect on that period of my life so fondly because of the bond I feel with my brothers and my sisters.

Just as with Pete and his paper round, I've got special recollections for each of my siblings. Wendy, for example, would frequently be the one to do 'girly' things with me. Whether painting my nails or brushing my hair, she was the one who could always be relied on to show so much love. She would cuddle me when I cried and gently wipe my knees when I fell. With such a big age difference between us – more than twelve years – she was more of a mother to me than a sister. Those early years laid the groundwork for our relationship and she is still the one I turn to when I'm sad now. Wendy would read to me endlessly, pretty much on demand, and I would sit on her lap for hours or snuggle up under her arm while she told me stories by Enid Blyton. *Cherry Tree Farm*, *Naughty Amelia Jane* and *The Magic Faraway Tree* were my favourites. I felt so happy and completely safe when my biggest sister wrapped me in her world of hugs and stories. She always read to me with such feeling and it gave me a love of books that has never left me; they are a refuge during difficult times.

When the older girls left school, further education wasn't something that was expected or encouraged – the pressure was on to get a paying job that would contribute to the household and relieve some of our financial burdens. My older sisters all went to work in what are commonly known in Stoke as the 'pot banks', the Staffordshire factories famous for producing pottery. I remember Jill and Wendy bringing home an assortment of clay cup handles, still soft, that I would wet and play with for hours, pretending that I too was a part of this fascinating grown-up production line.

At least once a year, we would travel to the house of my paternal grandparents in Haughton Green. They lived in a three-storey townhouse that was one of our favourite places in the world. We all loved going there. The warm and cosy smell would envelop you as soon as you walked in, as would Grandma, who was there with instant hugs, her soft skin smelling sweet from the baking that she was constantly doing. The house was always immaculate, and I loved the fact that it was 'upside down', with the living area and kitchen upstairs. Downstairs, there were patio doors leading onto the back garden, and a smaller living room that Grandad would sit in to watch TV. Their house was full of pretty little things, which made it so homely and special. In the main living room upstairs, there was a big fluffy sheepskin rug behind the sofa that I would lie on after dinner while the grown-ups talked. On the fireplace was a little stuffed tabby cat with green glass eyes that I would lay next to me and pet as if it were real. In the toilet upstairs, the loo roll was stored beneath a doll's knitted skirt: these hideous decorations are seen as something out of the Ark nowadays, a real cliché, but they seemed the height of sophistication to me back then.

Dinner was always spectacular. Grandma was an amazing cook and made everything from scratch. There would be a freshly baked apple pie and lots of other mouth-watering goodies. While the adults had a cup of tea I would have one in a little tiny china cup with its own little saucer and an illustration of Noddy on it; drinking carefully from it always made me feel grown up and special, which I'm sure was the aim.

After dinner, Grandad would go down and sit in his armchair and watch the sport on telly. In the corner of the room was a huge sideboard that had loads of toys in it, kept specially for when we came to visit. Michelle and I would play with the contents while Grandad sat glued to the TV, then go outside to play hide-and-seek.

Grandma and Grandad both tried to make everything special, really. When it was time to leave they would stand at the front door and hug us all goodbye, pressing 50p pieces into our hands as we left, ensuring that we went to the car with beaming smiles. One of my greatest wishes would be to have known my grandparents better and for longer, but, being the youngest of a large family, that wasn't to be. They passed away when I was fifteen, within weeks of each other. My maternal grandmother had died of kidney failure just a few weeks after giving birth to my mum. Her father had remarried but he died before I was born. I know the relationship between my mum and her father and step-grandma had not been a happy one.

When I was around six years old, my eldest sister Wendy got married. It was a big white church wedding, a huge affair for our family. Michelle and I were bridesmaids, wearing powder blue dresses with puffball sleeves and matching mob-caps. I hated that cap; it was like wearing a cloth shower cap and the elastic dug into my head – but we all suffer as bridesmaids, I guess. I remember sitting at the long table after the wedding breakfast and being asked to stand for the toast – I proclaimed loudly that I didn't want to as I wasn't hungry any more and didn't have room for toast!

After the wedding, Wendy set up home with her new husband and I spent lots of time there. It was a place of absolute luxury to me, having things that I wasn't accustomed to, such as a garage, fitted carpets and a kitchen big enough to have a dining table. Everything seemed so new and clean and I loved visiting, spending hours in the big empty garage at the side of the house that Wendy set up with deckchairs, tea sets and picnic things. It was like having a tiny house of my own in comparison to the crowding at home.

Another happy memory I have is of the one and only holiday we had as family; with so many of us and so little money to go around, we weren't in a position to have luxuries like that regularly, but when I was around seven we were told that we were all going to Butlins at Barry Island in Wales. Even Wendy came with her husband; only Jill didn't join our family gang as she was nearly eighteen by this time and had her own social life to be getting on with. I can remember to this day the excitement that I felt packing my things in the suitcase. I had even been bought new clothes, which was very rare. I especially remember a two-piece patterned bikini, bright blue with frills round the edge of the knickers and the two little triangles that made up the top. I also became the owner of some beautiful red and white strappy sandals that I absolutely adored. I thought they were the most gorgeous shoes that had ever existed and clearly remember, when we came back, wearing them to school, proudly watching my feet as I was skipping, thinking how envious my friends would be of my amazing new shoes. It's the only time I can remember getting new clothes at that stage of my life.

I remember setting off from our house to Barry Island, with the car loaded for the journey, arguing as to who wasn't sitting in the middle of the back seat. In my mind's eye, I can still see my best friend, my next-door neighbour, Mandy, waving to me from her bedroom window as we drove off for our adventure. I had a wonderful time, but I found out years later that few others in the family did; at my tender age, all I had to worry about was how I was going to spend my pocket money and when we were going to the beach.

We were allowed to go off on our own during the day. This time was spent at the fairground and on the beach making sandcastles, eating junk and candyfloss. At night, I would wander around following Michelle, creeping into the ballroom-dancing classes, hiding behind the chairs at the back and laughing at the couples in their glitzy outfits as they twirled around the floor, before going back to our tiny chalet. I'd collapse on the sofa bed where I slept each night, exhausted at being up way past my bedtime.

There were lots of photos taken on that holiday that I looked back on over the years. One was of me with a life-sized teddy I loved and the old classic of me being buried up to my neck in the sand, a task that Pete had performed (and had forgotten to take his boots off when stamping the sand down on my knees!). I loved the beach more than anything, feeling free and looking at the sea, which I thought went on for ever. I still look back on that holiday with fond memories.

I have only fractured memories of other things that happened back then. I remember one particular birthday, one Christmas and snatches of other occasions, such as Sports Day at school in the summer. I also have a vivid memory of sunbathing on the grass in front of our house, wearing wellies and a big coat so that the grass didn't tickle my legs. These few memories are so broken and so few that they feel spiky with emotion, the ragged edges of what they represent made so much bigger than the reality of the events themselves.

There is the winter morning when I opened the back door of our house to come face-to-face with a wall of snow that was higher than me, then trekking to school in my wellies, the snow up to my waist, only to have to turn round again because the school had been closed due to the weather. I went home, giddy and excited to have an unexpected day off, like all kids back then when every winter's morning was a new opportunity for the sweet possibility of an unscheduled day making snowballs and snowmen.

There is the Christmas that I got everything my heart desired: a beautiful shiny new doll's pram, complete with dolly and bedding, a smart wooden desk with a lift-up lid and a shiny red stool. I pushed the pram up and down the lanes for years and had the desk until I left home. I think it was a particularly successful Christmas for me that year because my older sisters were all working and had been spoiling me, too. These memories have a dull ache to them, where the happiness mixes with the knowledge of what future winters, future Christmases would bring.

There are a few of these memories of that time of year – perhaps we remember better when there are external reference points to guide us, the snow, the cold – and they catch my breath now in the same way as living them did. I recall being allowed to eat my Christmas dinner sat at my desk. Two years after Wendy had left and got married, Jill followed suit, marrying and setting up home with a local lad who lived a few doors up from us (and who she is still married to). Babies came shortly after, Wendy having the first of her two sons and Jill eventually having four children in all, one girl and three boys. I used to stay at her house during the school holidays, and she would feed me up and make me laugh even while up to her neck in nappies. Never having experienced being an older sister myself, I was proud and ecstatic to be an auntie. I was only about eight and will never forget that feeling of holding my tiny nephews on my lap for the first time, scared that I might break them and marvelling at their doll-like fingers and toes. These are memories that stick, and I need that, I need some of the good stuff.

Overall, my childhood, up to the age of eight, was one of contentment. I felt safe, secure, loved and part of a family. This was, however, despite my mother, not because of her, and mostly thanks to my brothers and sisters. I know that, within families, different members can have different recollections of the same events and experiences, so I am aware that this is all being filtered through my personal lens, but I wish so much that I could go back and grab every lovely memory and relive every happy experience from those early years, not any one magical moment but all the little ones: playing happily without a care in the world, taking for granted the fact that I was loved and cared for, wandering up and down the lanes playing with my best friend or brothers and sisters or even just by myself.

As time went on, I felt as if I only really ever saw Mum in passing. Dad was always there, in the garden, or I'd be sitting on his lap in the lounge. It's not that Mum was horrible during that time, it was that she only ever came alive when she was working behind the bar. If I was ever taken there to pick her up, she was so vivacious – not like my mum at all. Sometimes, on summer nights, when it was still pretty much light at closing time, Dad would pick me up if I was struggling to sleep, pop me in the car and say, 'Let's get Mum.' I thought it was such an adventure, but I know now that when we got there, and he would tell me to sit while he went to look for her, it wasn't right. On those nights she wasn't in the pub finishing off her shift – she was off with someone and he had to drag her back. I'd sometimes see him getting her from another car. They'd come back to ours and she would often say words I remember so clearly.

'What the fuck have you brought her for?'

Dad would tell her to be quiet, smile at me, and we'd go home. I didn't know then that she was with other men. I didn't really know any of it.

But I was happy. I had Dad and I had my brothers and sisters. I had those long summer days and nights, and I would love to go back to them. Perhaps, more than anything, I would go back to the days when my love of horses was an innocent thing. I used to trot up and down pretending I was riding a horse of my own, stopping every now and then to get off and let it eat grass and drink water. My imagination has always been the only thing I've ever needed to occupy myself, hence my love of books, and as an adult I'm still quite a solitary person most of the time; looking back at the early days, it's the only time in my life that my head was as clear as a child's should be, and this was especially true when I had my imaginary horse. When my mind wasn't full of worry, guilt, fear, sadness, anger and self-loathing, the many negative emotions that over the coming years would make me feel as if my head was going to explode, I would just think of horses. Horses, horses, horses. That's what I want to go back to. Innocence. Love. A time before hell.

CHAPTER 2

A Different World

I REMEMBER LEAVING the house with Mum and Michelle, getting on bus after bus and travelling for what seemed like an eternity. I would have been around eight years old.

'Where are we going?' I asked. I knew that it was too far to be my grandparents' house, but I still hoped that it would be somewhere nice – perhaps we were meeting them somewhere for the day?

'Manchester,' snapped Mum.

'Why are we going there?' We had never been there before, and it seemed like such a long journey already.

'We're going to see your Uncle Graham,' she told me.

'Who? Who's that?' I asked, having never heard of Uncle Graham.

'We're going to Ashton,' she told me, sighing. 'Graham's

my brother; we're staying with him for a couple of weeks. He's got a pub – we'll live there for a bit.'

That seemed quite an adventure as we rarely got taken anywhere, but I don't remember asking more questions such as, Why were we going there? Was Dad coming later? What about my other siblings? Why now?

After travelling for most of the day – and cold, tired and hungry by that point – we arrived that evening. It was a big white pub, set back from the main road and surrounded by a car park. The huge sign on the front read 'The Odd Whim Inn' and was accompanied by a picture of a witch on a broomstick. As I followed Mum in through the bubbled glass doors, we hit a wall of sound. There was chatting and music and the tinkling of fruit machines. The smell of beer, food and cigarette smoke was strong in the air as a man walked towards us. He was tall and quite handsome, with twinkling blue eyes, and he bore a very strong resemblance to my mother, so I assumed he was Uncle Graham. He threw his arms round us, hugging and kissing me and Mum and Michelle, then took us over to some people who were sitting at the bar.

'This is my baby sister!' he announced, which I found hilarious – but also strange, as, until that day, I hadn't been aware that my mum even had any siblings. After introductions, we were taken upstairs, and I was surprised to find a fairly large, homely looking flat. It was warm and cosy, and Uncle Graham had obviously gone to a lot of trouble to make it nice, as well as preparing a lovely meal for our arrival. We met his son and daughter – our cousins – who lived with him during the week (they stayed with their mum at weekends); we spent a nice evening getting to know each other and, although I found this sudden discovery of family a little strange, the welcome was undeniably a warm one. I felt – even though no one had said this – that we wouldn't be there for long, and this compensated for the unfamiliarity. The sleeping arrangements were a little cramped, but as a large family we were used to that. Michelle, Mum and I all squeezed up and shared my cousin Mandy's bed, while she slept in a put-me-up bed at the foot of what was now 'ours'.

The visit lasted for much longer than I'd expected, and we ended up staying there for a few weeks, getting to know our cousins, playing hide-and-seek downstairs when the pub was closed and visiting the huge markets in Ashton. Mum spent most of her time in the bar, helping to serve, chatting to customers and having a drink. All in all, it was quite a pleasant time and, before leaving, we made arrangements for Mandy to come and visit us in Stoke in a few months' time. She was roughly the same age as Michelle and they had become firm friends. I'd missed my dad and brothers and sisters a lot though, and I was so glad to be going home.

Looking back, there must have been something happening at home. We had been gone for almost a month, and that visit had come out of nowhere, with Mum choosing to take only me and Michelle, so I can't imagine it all went smoothly between her and Dad when we got back, but I was either oblivious to it or have forgotten as the next thing that sticks in my mind was Mandy's visit, some time later, which came and went. I don't remember much about it except for not wanting to go to school in case I missed something; I can't even remember where she slept. Not long afterwards, however, Mum, Michelle and I were heading back up to Manchester again for another visit. Knowing what to expect this time, I was looking forward to it: seeing everyone again, having an endless supply of fizzy pop from the pub and a few weeks off school.

Once we arrived things were much the same, with Mum mostly drinking in the bar, and Michelle spending a lot of her time with Mandy. My cousins would play with me but, being so much older, it was probably a pain for them, although they were always good-natured about it. The days turned into weeks, the weeks turned into a month and I was starting to really miss my dad and siblings. I constantly wondered when we would be going home. Eventually I became so desperate that one day, as Mum was walking through the lounge, I asked the question outright.

'When are we going home?'

She didn't miss a step.

'Never,' she coldly replied, and carried on walking without so much as looking at me.

A Different World

I felt sick to my stomach. My throat was tight with shock and the effort of trying not to cry. I didn't know if she meant it, but I had a bad feeling and couldn't even contemplate the thought of staying there and never going home. I didn't mention Mum's response for a few days afterwards, hoping that she'd tell me she'd changed her mind or that she was joking, but nothing was said, and I finally plucked up the courage to ask.

'Did you mean what you said?' I asked, gingerly. 'Are we really never going home? I want to – I want to go home so much.'

Immediately, she flew into a rage, as if she had been waiting for me to ask, screaming and shouting at me.

'I needn't have brought you in the first place!' she yelled. 'If it wasn't for me, you would have been put into a fucking children's home. Best place for you!'

I was speechless, but she had only just started.

'I stayed with your dad for the last twenty years because of you kids, so you can fucking well do something for me for a change. We're staying. Get used to it.'

She started to walk away, obviously still fuming, before changing her mind and coming back into the room.

'You better be fucking grateful, do you understand? It's your fault, the fault of ALL of you, that I have been completely bloody miserable for so long – I could have been happy, I could have dumped you all and gone off to have a life of my own, but I didn't because there were so bloody many of you all. He would never have coped, you know that?'

I didn't.

I knew none of it. I loved my dad and I had thought he loved us.

'He would have put you all in a children's home; so I sacrificed MY happiness for you lot. You fucking owe me. The least you can do is stop complaining.'

There was a part of me that wanted to ask why she'd kept having kids if it meant that she felt so sad with us all, but she clearly didn't want me to do anything but shut up, so I did. And that was how I discovered I would never be going home. I wouldn't see my dad again until I was fourteen years old.

I couldn't stop thinking about what we'd left behind. I missed Jill and the way she could always make me laugh so easily. I missed Andy's hippy hair and his bad teeth, his long suede embroidered coat and the smell of patchouli oil that hung around him. I missed the vocal, outgoing nature of Pete. I missed them all. You get pigeonholed in a big family, and I thought of all the roles they had played in my life so far and it broke my heart to think that I'd lost that.

I frequently got upset over the coming weeks and months as the reality of the situation hit home; this only annoyed and irritated her.

'What the fuck's up with you now?' she would say

on seeing me crying again. When I'd say that I missed my dad or anything to do with my old life she would instantly become enraged.

'It's all about you, isn't it? Well, I've got news for you, you're no one fucking special. I've given up enough of my life for you lot, now it's my turn.'

She would repeat this phrase many times over the years ahead or whenever I was showing signs of being unhappy. It was always, 'You're no one special.' I didn't think that I was special; I just didn't understand how she expected me to forget my life up to that point and pretend it had never existed.

It soon became apparent that I could no longer continue to hold out any hopes of returning to what I still thought of as home; nor was I allowed to mention my father without there being World War Three. If I ever did bring these things up, she would just snarl that she was 'never going back to the fucking bastard' and that I didn't know him at all. All in all, life was much more bearable if I didn't mention him.

Mentioning my brothers and sisters was a different matter, mainly because Mum intended to continue a relationship with them I suppose. I'm sure she also must have known that they wouldn't have readily accepted such a loss of contact with me and Michelle. If ever I mentioned missing them, she'd say that they'd be able to come and visit. But I didn't want them to visit, I wanted to go back to my house and my school where I knew everyone and where things were as I'd always known them to be. I wanted my best friend who I'd known all my life and who lived just next door to me. I wanted my toys and books and belongings, and all the people I didn't want to live without. It wasn't just the tangible things I missed: it was a way of life.

Things in a city were very different from what I was used to. I had been brought up in a small village where everybody knew and looked out for each other, where I felt safe playing out alone and could wander through fields stroking cows and horses. My new environment was a stark contrast and came as something of a culture shock: outside the four walls of the pub seemed to be a sea of concrete, where there were no trees or animals or peace. Children of my own age that I met were different; they were far more streetwise than me and would laugh at my naivety, and they made fun of my accent as soon as I opened my mouth, saying that I sounded like I had a plum in my mouth. They would mock it, and me, at every opportunity.

Eventually I gave up hope that things would change. It wasn't long before the unavoidable happened and I had to start a new school. Mum decided to send me to the local Catholic junior school and Michelle to the Catholic secondary, even though we hadn't been brought up in that religion at all and there was a Church of England school right across the road from the pub. Uncle Graham was a regular churchgoer and, since our arrival, we'd reluctantly been dragged along every Sunday. Mum embraced this wholeheartedly and mentioned it frequently; I think she saw it as a way of raising her social standing without having to do an awful lot other than sit in church once a week. The rest of her behaviour certainly didn't adhere to the rules of the faith – or any other, come to that. So, I suppose that's where the school thing came from, another way of alluding to respectability without actually having to do anything herself, never mind how alien it was to us.

We weren't consulted, only told that Michelle would have to start having some religious instruction at the local church and that this was just how things were now. I was more put out at the prospect of having to wear a uniform, as I didn't really understand what being Catholic meant back then. I did worry that it might mean being taught by nuns holding rosary beads and spending all day in silence, but Uncle Graham laughingly reassured me that this wasn't the case. I was still desperately missing my friends and family from home but accepted what I was told, thinking that things couldn't possibly get any worse. My innocent eight-year-old mind thought that my life was as bad as it could be, being suddenly removed from everything and everyone that I loved. I had no way of imagining the horrors to come, or realising that all the happy memories of my childhood so far were to be all I would be left with for ever.

31

Though Uncle Graham was kind at first, he had some habits and rules that I found really strange. We were made to eat bread with every meal while sat at the table and weren't allowed to leave anything on our plates. While this had been the loose rule at home, the encouragement to eat everything that comes with being in a large family that can't afford waste, it certainly wasn't forced upon us to the point of making us sick as it was here. At home, there was always someone else more than willing to eat your leftovers, whereas Uncle Graham would sometimes have me sitting there for ages, telling me to eat, telling me to finish my food, staring at me and making it clear that he would win this battle. Naturally, the more he insisted, the less I felt like eating. On some occasions, even Mum intervened and told him to let me leave the table, but he always overruled her and insisted that I continue to keep forcing the food down.

One time, he tried to get me to try a chunk of tripe; the white fatty-looking piece of flesh made me want to gag just looking at it and I didn't want to even consider it. The more I refused, the angrier he got, until I was in tears. Eventually he held my nose and, when I had to open it, shoved it in my mouth. As I felt the cold squidginess hit my tongue I started to retch.

'Swallow it! Swallow it!' Uncle Graham screamed, standing over me, like a man possessed.

I managed to put it under my tongue and on demand show him my seemingly empty mouth.

A Different World

'See, it wasn't that bad!' he shouted, triumphantly.

As soon as he turned to go, pleased that his mission had been accomplished, I spat it out and threw it behind the bread bin, where it was left to fester. I never went near the stuff again and still can't stand the sight of it; it conjures up Uncle Graham's face looking demonic in his attempts to make me eat the stuff. There was always a bit of me on my guard with Uncle Graham after that.

Life eventually settled into some sort of routine; not a routine that I liked but a routine nevertheless. I started my new school and hated it. For weeks I had to be carried in, literally kicking and screaming, while the other kids looked on in amazement. Not a great start. I was instantly looked on as some kind of weirdo, but the strangeness of everything and the desire to go back to my old life were overwhelming and I didn't know how to cope. In hindsight I needed someone to sit down and explain things properly and reassure me, but that wasn't going to happen, so my distress and confusion continued.

The school was a lot different from my old one: it was much bigger, it smelled different and the children were already in their little cliques and were very different from my old friends. The desire to be back with them was almost too much to bear. Once I had settled down a bit and accepted that I had to go, I did get talking to some of the other kids, but it soon became apparent that I didn't have much in common with them. Most of them were from well-off middle-class families with smart houses, and their parents were professionals and very friendly with the teachers at the school. There was mild interest at first in the fact that I had a different accent and lived in a pub, with a mixture of curiosity and awkwardness when they discovered that my parents were separated, as it was by no means the norm back then. This was something else that set me apart from the others. A couple of girls had dads who had died, but this was to be viewed differently and was somehow more socially acceptable than my situation. I would go to school miserable and return home miserable; it never got any better.

Home, as I grudgingly called it, was much the same. After school I would have dinner and look on as Mum dolled herself up ready for the evening shift. I remember watching every painstaking application of make-up as I had with my sisters, and would be amazed at the transformation, thinking she looked so pretty and glamorous. For the rest of the evening she and Uncle Graham would be downstairs 'working', although, in hindsight, this mainly involved standing at the bar chatting to customers while drinking glass after glass of brandy. We would always be left to our own devices, not even being made to go to bed, so I would often be tired at school. Sometimes we would be allowed downstairs for an hour or two after they had drunk enough to relax and not care if we were around them or not. As time passed I started going downstairs more often, and without permission, always finding Mum draped all over some man or other, rarely the same man twice, and obviously roaring drunk.

I wasn't comfortable with this new mother who would wear revealing clothes and flirt with any man willing to talk to her. I wasn't used to it and felt upset and embarrassed. In later life, I was told that she had regular affairs throughout her marriage to my dad, though I don't and can't know the truth of this. It was apparent anyhow that things had been less than harmonious; it was just that I'd been protected from it then in a way that I no longer was.

I was still in an emotionally raw state. It would only take a song to come on the jukebox that reminded me of my brothers and sisters to get me in floods of tears. I'd cry in the bedroom for hours. Part of my feelings of injustice came from the fact that I couldn't see any evidence of Mum even wanting me there, so I didn't understand why she had made me come. She seemed to resent me, and said I was 'a fucking nuisance', so why had she brought me? If I could have talked to her about things and heard that she felt the same way it might have helped, but she never showed any signs of feeling the way I did; she rarely talked about any of the family and certainly never appeared to be unhappy. Any time she was down was usually due to her involvement with some man not going as she wanted it to.

Uncle Graham was also very flirtatious. A good-looking man, he always had an admirer hanging around him, and had started to go out of his way to keep embarrassing me. I started to develop quite early and was very self-conscious about it. Uncle Graham, however, found it hilarious to keep saying 'Your boobs are growing!' at every opportunity and in front of everyone, strangers, customers or whoever. Inside, I would feel as if I could die of embarrassment.

Mum would stand there laughing.

'You'll be glad of them one day!' she'd shriek, pointing at my chest in front of all the men in the bar. Her philosophy was to have as much flesh on display as possible at any time. The more you showed, the more desirable you were. Any other female was a threat, especially if they were attractive: their beauty automatically meant that they wouldn't be a nice person. They would be self-absorbed and bitchy, and either stab you in the back or try to take your man from you. Everything, in fact, that she was and did. The only people to be trusted in her unspoken opinion were either far less attractive than her or very fat – she spoke of other women horribly and had no time for them.

Graham, I think, was basically a good person – apart from the comments about my 'development'. He was funny and lively and he loved his kids. They spent weekends with their mum, which I think was because he worked during the week. When they came back from hers, she would send sweets for me and Michelle and I liked her. I don't know why they split up, but I do know that Graham could go from being the loveliest man on the planet to almost psychotic in the blink of an eye. If he'd been drinking too much, he could kick off over a slice of bread that hadn't been eaten. He wasn't the problem though – it was Mum. She and Graham were together all the time, a real double act. She was always in his room and they were very tactile together. When they hugged, it was very intense, and I would see them touching in a way that seemed odd for brother and sister. She was always jealous of any attention he got in the bar, even though she was going through men like used tissues. There was a constant source, and she seemed to love that.

Mum had always liked to doll herself up, but it was on a different level now. I watched the whole process whenever I could, as it fascinated me. The pub opened at 11 a.m. and shut at 3 p.m., so she would have one face and one outfit for that. It would be open again from 5–11 p.m. and she would have to get ready for that session too. She would begin an hour before, putting her fine hair in rollers while she did her make-up. I guess she was still young, only in her mid-thirties, and this was really the first time she had ever been single. She had her freedom, in her own way, and she dressed for it, showing as much skin as she could, with her chest hoicked up as far as it could go. I would be embarrassed by that, but if

I ever said anything, she'd reply, 'I'll put nipple tassels on them if you're not careful – see what you think of that, Little Miss Prude.'

All she wanted was alcohol and men – and she had both in abundance. She started drinking from the minute they opened, then she and Graham would sleep until it was time for her to get her make-up on again for the night shift. They slept in his room on those afternoons and she would say it was in case we needed to use our shared bedroom. I wonder, I really do.

What I do know is that it was a toxic environment. Alcohol, jealousy and a complete displacement from everything I had ever known. I finally had to accept this different world was my world now. This was it – I wasn't going back 'home'.

CHAPTER 3

Grateful

MUM AND UNCLE Graham were drinking more and more heavily. They would have a large drink in their hands from the moment they opened the pub until the end of the night when they locked up. They would laugh about the fact that during the course of the evening they'd finished one bottle and would be opening another. They'd carry on drinking long after closing time, sitting until the early hours, sometimes with bar staff and a few chosen regulars, or sometimes on their own. Weekends would always be the same and, as the pub was at its busiest, we would, as always, be left to our own devices.

Saturday lunch was a ritual, home-made pea and ham soup with sandwiches – made by the cellar man actually, not them – and then I'd settle down for the evening's television, trying to drown out the music and noise from downstairs. My favourite was *The Cannon and Ball Show*, which I looked forward to all week, knowing it was the one time when I'd forget everything else and laugh so hard that I cried. It probably sounds ridiculous nowadays, when you can access any programme you like at any time you want, but back then, there was a comfort in knowing there was one thing every week that could make you laugh without fail even if you did have to wait for it.

At weekends the pub was full and a favourite haunt of bikers. Mum was in her element, showing maximum cleavage and flirting with everyone around her, desperate to get noticed. Sometimes I'd come downstairs and get really worried when I couldn't see her. I'd find Uncle Graham to ask where she was, and he would say that she had either 'gone for a ride' or 'gone for some fresh air.' With butterflies in my stomach, I'd go upstairs to stare out of the windows overlooking the car park, waiting for her to come back, worried that she might have gone for good. Eventually she'd appear, stumbling out of someone's car, and I'd just be relieved that she had come back at all, being far too young to properly contextualise what was going on.

However, over time, Mum's sexual encounters became more and more obvious and considerably more varied.

After we'd been sent to the Catholic schools, we were told we were to be baptised. For godparents Mum chose two customers from the pub, a husband and wife who were part of the biker crowd and ran a joke shop in the town centre. I'd seen them around the pub and had visited their shop a couple of times since she had become friends with them, and we had been told to refer to them as Auntie and Uncle. They had a reputation as hard nuts and for being partial to a fight. Before long, Mum was often cosying up between the two of them and rumours were rife that they were having threesomes. It certainly seemed a strange situation: Mum and the other woman would sit on either side of the man, while he had an arm around each of them, often with his hands down their tops. His wife was obviously okay with this bizarre spectacle but, given that most people were terrified of them both (maybe of Mum too), nobody dared comment. I think that, as Mum usually disliked other women so much, there must have been something to the rumours, as she would ordinarily have been calling the wife all the names under the sun.

There were also rumours that the man had been in prison for taking indecent pictures of juveniles, though I didn't learn this until later. However, there were two occasions when, walking behind me, he had slid his hand up my skirt and tickled my legs. Nothing more sinister had happened but, given that I was only eight years of age, it was highly inappropriate and made me feel very uncomfortable and embarrassed. Of course, the constant message from Mum was that the only sort of attention worth having from men was of the sexual kind. If you weren't happy with this, then you were some sort of frigid prude who thought that you were better than everyone else. Quantity over quality was definitely the message, no matter how inappropriate the attention.

I can recall so many times during my early teens when, looking older than my years as I did, I would get attention from twenty- and thirty-year-olds. Rather than warning people off and being naturally protective like most mothers would, Mum found it highly exciting and flattering, as if it was in some way a compliment to her, and would encourage their dubious attentions. If I didn't feel the same then she would mock me, saying that I fancied myself and thought that I was Lady Muck. She'd use the same phrase that she had from when I was eight years old and grown men were leering at my chest:

'Your shit still stinks like the rest of us,' she would sneer.

Her flirtations knew no boundaries; there were no age limits or moral no-go areas. Seventeen or seventy, she didn't care, as long as she thought there was a remote possibility they might reciprocate. The husbands of friends, the sons of friends, the husbands of neighbours all received her attention, her offering it on a plate. Of course, they played a part in it – it was their choice whether to take the offer up – but that was the environment I grew up in and that was how I was

42

raised to think of sex. Women had one thing to trade, and only male attention mattered. My mum, 'good old Glo', would always be there, dirty laugh and dirty jokes at the ready, never a thought for other women unless it was to insult them, always judging herself and her daughters by how many men were after them. As we got older – and my sisters were already seeing this – over the years most of their boyfriends and husbands were treated to an eyeful as well as the embarrassment of her suggestive behaviour and innuendos. She had absolutely no scruples when it came to betraying other women.

The day before my ninth birthday will remain in my mind for the rest of my life. It had been an emotional day. I was feeling very low and heartbroken to be facing my first birthday without my brothers, sisters and Dad. I'd spent most of the day trying my best not to cry and antagonise Mum, but a song had come on the radio – 'Sugar Baby Love' by the Rubettes – and it just broke me. It was a song that Pete used to play over and over again in his bedroom, and the very sound of it made me realise just how much I missed my big brother, just how much I missed all of them. It opened the floodgates and once I started crying, I couldn't stop.

Everything we'd ever done together was swimming through my mind. I knew without a doubt that things would never be like that again. I don't ever remember crying as much and it was one of the lowest moments I'd ever experienced up to that point. In fact, that song still makes me feel emotional to this day.

I was exhausted from crying and didn't know what to do next. I had eaten the compulsory soup and sandwiches that the cellar man made me every weekend and was sat on the sofa waiting for my favourite programmes. I was hoping that Cannon and Ball would prove me wrong in thinking that I would never laugh or smile again, and all I needed to do was hang on until the programme started later that evening.

Shortly after dinner, Uncle Graham brought a man upstairs. This man and Mum threw their arms around each other. I didn't know who he was and couldn't remember ever seeing him before, so just assumed that he was one of the regular customers from downstairs. He was his fifties and, the closer I looked at him, the more I could see that he looked extremely like my mum. In truth, he was quite strange-looking with long white straggly hair and a weathered face. He wore a dark donkey jacket, the sort of coat that council workers used to wear, and was finally introduced as Uncle Phil.

The term 'uncle' was used very loosely during those days and could apply to any of Mum's male friends; however this time it seemed that he really was my uncle. He was another of her older brothers who I hadn't known existed. Uncle Phil stayed for the afternoon talking with Mum and Uncle Graham until they went downstairs for the evening shift in the pub.

Grateful

I was curled up on the sofa feeling emotionally drained and watching Cannon and Ball when he came and sat next to me. There was plenty of room, and even another free sofa in the room, but he squashed right up to me and put his arm around my back, pulling me in to him. I felt uneasy immediately but was also getting used to people I thought of as complete strangers being overfamiliar. I was always told to give customers and Mum's male friends a kiss or made to sit on their knee, when I didn't know them from Adam. At least this one had the advantage of being family.

As I watched telly, Uncle Phil moved in even closer towards me. I was so young, but I had already experienced so much unwanted male attention from customers, all of it laughed at by Mum, all of it seen by her as a reflection of her sexual attractiveness. But surely this one – this man, who was my uncle – surely this one didn't mean anything?

I wasn't in two minds for long.

He leered at me and slipped his hand down my top, squeezing my barely developed breast and pinching my nipple.

'Is that nice? Do you like that?' he whispered in my ear.

No, I didn't like it, and of course it wasn't 'nice'! I froze with fear and felt myself burning up from shame and embarrassment. Not feeling able to move or speak, I didn't know what to do. I was in shock. I fixed my eyes on the TV, wishing him away from me as hard as I could, wishing he would get his filthy hands off me. He kept touching me, kept nipping me and stroking me, as I refused to speak, refused to interact with him.

Then . . . then, I heard the sound of him opening the zip of his jeans as he wriggled close to me. He reached across, grabbed my hand and pulled it towards him, trying to force it down his pants. I felt the coarse wiriness of his pubic hair – though I didn't know what it was at the time – and, holding my breath with fear, I snatched my hand away as hard as I could. I hoped it would leave him in no doubt that I didn't welcome this in any way, but he didn't stop. Slipping his arm underneath me, Uncle Phil manoeuvred in such a way that my legs were bent beneath me. He then moved my knickers to one side and began to play with my private area, whispering in my ear the whole time.

'Is that nice?' he kept saying. 'Is that nice?'

He then pushed his fingers into me, his long dirty nails scratching inside where no one should have been in the first place. I was terrified and couldn't believe what was happening. I felt so sick, I thought that if I opened my mouth the vomit would come up, so I sat frozen to the spot with my eyes fixed on the TV, watching but taking nothing in. I wanted to close my eyes and wake up back in Stoke with my family – either that or never wake up again. But life doesn't work like that. I was in a nightmare, but with complete awareness that it was happening.

That was the day before my ninth birthday. My life had gone from being totally miserable to intolerable in such a short space of time. I was confused; I knew it was wrong but also knew somehow that if I said anything it would be me making a fuss again. Me, the one who wanted to go home; me, the one who spoiled things by being miserable and wanting to be with my dad and brothers and sisters. Me, the one who thought her shit didn't smell. Me, who should be so grateful that Mum had brought me to this hellhole, away from everything and everyone I loved.

I felt that even if I did tell her what Uncle Phil had done she wouldn't find it a big deal and would make me out to be the one with a problem. Looking back, I had no firm grounds for feeling like that at the time, except for the intuition that children often have about a situation without knowing why.

I didn't say anything, and that hellish night became a regular way of life. Every weekend Uncle Phil would visit, the loving brother and uncle making up for lost time with his family, and every weekend would follow the same pattern. He would sit on the sofa and, patting the seat next to him, would tell me to come and sit beside him. If I didn't, or tried to make an excuse, Mum would be right in there.

'What the fuck's up with you?' she'd snarl. 'Just sit down!' I would look at her imploringly, longing for her to be a normal mother and see that I was terrified. But she would scowl at me and make some comment about me being awkward, until I would go and sit down just to avoid her anger and disapproval.

No matter how I sat, Uncle Phil always managed the same thing. It was his signature manoeuvre – who knows how he had honed it? In one practised movement, he would slip his arm around me, pulling me in to him and bringing my legs up beneath me. Then, putting his hand underneath where it couldn't be seen, he would pull my knickers to the side and push his fingers into me, stroking and prodding me. If ever I tried to shift, his nails would dig in tighter, making me want to cry out and making it impossible for me to move. It was bad enough the first time when I was alone, but as he could now only get me to sit next to him when someone else was there, it soon became the case that it was regularly happening in front of other people, right under their noses. Everyone would be sat talking, watching TV or whatever, and he'd be chatting away with them, about world politics, the price of bread, anything, while all the time I was imprisoned under his arm and he was slowly taking my childhood away.

I would be frozen, not believing that others couldn't see what he was doing. A small part of me actually thought that if he was doing it in front of them, maybe they did know and somehow it was okay. But, if it was okay, why was it making me feel so bad? This led to my gradual belief that everyone knew what he was doing, and it was just one of those things that wasn't to be discussed; it was just me who had a problem with it. Looking back, maybe he got a kick out of getting away with it right under everyone's nose, or maybe it was just desperation and a total lack of self-control.

There is no doubt that Uncle Phil was a bit strange. His presence used to make my heart pound with worry, for obvious reasons, but even to the average onlooker he would have come across as a bit eccentric and bizarre, with his weathered face and long white hair. He had a somewhat bohemian style, shall we say, often wearing no socks, no shirt in summer, and sporting lilac corduroys and very feminine clothes. He had strange, nervous mannerisms. He would talk very quickly and spit while speaking, saliva hovering in the corner of his mouth. He was not someone who, had his behaviour been found out, would have had people saying, 'I would never have guessed!' He was, in fact, a complete cliché of an oddball. Despite this, he managed to keep a job as an engineer for the GPO, who ran the telephone network in those days.

One day, I heard Mum and one of the barmaids chatting about him. The other woman was questioning why Phil had never settled down and had a family. Mum said that he'd once been engaged to a girl named Margaret while he was in his twenties.

'They were engaged to be married when Margaret was tragically knocked down and killed in a road accident,' said Mum. 'She was everything to him. After that, he was never the same and was always a bit funny. It's heartbreaking really. Poor Phil.'

This all sounded terribly tragic and romantic to me in my young head and my heart went out to him. Though it never excused what he was doing, in my confused brain, it went some way to explaining why he was the way he was. It was many, many years later, after having heard Mum relate the story in dramatic fashion a thousand times, that I learned the truth – she had lied countless times to protect him (and herself). The truth was, he himself confessed many years later that, yes, he had once been engaged, and she was called Margaret. However, her downfall hadn't been in a road accident; she had discovered that her fiancé had been more interested in her twelve-year-old sister. Margaret had called the wedding off when she realised what Phil was.

I wish she had done more. I know that's wrong, I know that the only people responsible for abusing children are the abusers, but I can't help but wonder *what if*? What if Margaret had reported him? What if Uncle Graham had paid more attention? What if one of the bar staff or the customers or the cellar man, or anyone, anyone at all, had noticed the uncle who sat too close to the little girl? The frozen, silenced little girl, with her knees pulled up so that the uncle could steal her childhood from her in full view of everyone, everyone who kept their eyes on the TV, their minds somewhere else. Everyone who thought that little girl was just stuck-up or miserable or sad because she wasn't getting what she wanted.

'Be fucking grateful,' Mum would tell me whenever it even looked as if I might be about to say something that she could interpret as 'moaning'. 'Be fucking grateful for what you've got, because I sacrificed my happiness for years for you.'

Gratitude, little Kate – push down the screams and the vomit and the terror. Try to forget the smell of him. His nails, his hands. The vile stench of his body, the horrific leer on his face. Be grateful, you little madam, be grateful.

CHAPTER 4

Growing pains

LIFE WENT ON. I still had very few friends at school and, on more than one occasion, ended up bursting into tears without even knowing why. I really would think I was okay, then, all of a sudden, the tears would come. Things like that didn't help me fit in any better. I didn't know, or couldn't admit to myself, what was wrong and why I was in a constant state of emotional turmoil. It was a mixture of so many things and, looking back, I don't think that there was anything right with my life at the time. I had come to accept the abuse I was now enduring on a regular basis. It was yet another part of my life that just had to be endured. Deep down, I believed that anything I had a problem with was just me being awkward; this was how I was always made to feel. I was at a very vulnerable age with no one to talk to about even the less traumatic things – school problems and teen problems – never mind the serious stuff that I refused to even acknowledge in my own mind.

I think that labels stick very quickly at that age and I was so used to being snarled at and belittled whenever I was sad or upset that I quickly learned to believe that I was indeed the silly, stroppy one and that the things happening to me were perfectly acceptable in everyone else's eyes. Mum's behaviour was now an increasing spiral of being drunk and all over a man, or in a state of deep depression, lying in bed for hours on end crying. Refusing to say why, she would tell me to go away when I'd pop my head around the door and ask her what was wrong, wanting to cuddle her. This was one of my first glimpses of the depression that she suffered with over the years; one of the few legacies I was to get from her.

I'll never know whether my affliction is a case of nature or nurture. If I'd had a happy, cosy childhood then I could have blamed it on a 'chemical imbalance', as the doctors describe it, but when there are so many things I could attribute it to – not least, some of the choices I've made along my journey into adulthood that are directly linked to what I endured as a child – who can say?

It was a miserable way to exist, but I was finally given some happy news when I was nine: my brother Andy was coming to live with us. This was brilliant for me. Although I'd never spent lots of time with Andy, as he tended to keep himself to himself and was eight years older than me, it was still a precious link to the life I had once known, which was fast becoming a distant memory. I couldn't wait to see him. Having no money, he hitchhiked the fifty-four miles from Stoke to Ashton. While it wasn't a big reunion, it was lovely to have him around. Uncle Phil got on really well with my elder brother and, although his presence didn't stop him touching me, he certainly seemed less inclined to while Andy was there and would take extra precautions, covering us with his coat and constantly shifting his position to make sure that nothing damning could be seen.

As soon as he arrived, Andy set out to look for work, having just left school. He was determined not to come back until he'd got a job. True to his word, after being gone for the whole day, he arrived back and said he'd been offered a training scheme with a tyre company. Mum's mood had also temporarily improved since Andy's arrival. She was comfortable with, and not threatened by, her sons as she was with her daughters, and it flattered her maternal ego that Andy had followed us. She seemed to think this proved that she was Mother of the Year material and had one up on my dad. The truth of it was that Andy and Dad had never been close, so it had probably only been a matter of time before he would follow us on.

By this time the pub was suffering badly; with Mum and Uncle Graham steadily drinking the pub's profits and fewer customers coming in, it was inevitable. Male customers were now bored with 'Good Time Glo'; most of them had had her and were on to the next offering at the next pub. Mum and Uncle Graham's drinking was out of control, and they were getting through several bottles of brandy a night between them. Uncle Graham had a stomach ulcer, and night after night he would come upstairs and spend ages throwing up in the bathroom, bringing up blood as the alcohol took effect on his damaged stomach.

At one point, he began hallucinating. Standing at the bar one early evening, he began swiping imaginary insects off the bar top, convinced they were swarming everywhere. The same night he kept asking me to go and remove an imaginary dog from under one of the tables, as it was bothering the customers who sat there. I went over, under Mum's instruction to play along, to go and pick up this invisible dog and take it outside, only for him to say ten minutes later, 'Quick Katie, it's back in, go and get rid of it!' As children we found this strange but hilarious; in hindsight he was obviously seriously ill. This bizarre spectacle was played out in front of the customers, so it was little wonder that numbers eventually dwindled given that management was totally losing the plot.

Eventually we were forced to move out. I remember things being packed up and the embarrassment of that piece of mouldy tripe that I'd spat out months before being found behind the bread bin (housework was evidently not a priority). Luckily, Uncle Graham was as bewildered as everyone else as it was unidentifiable; only I knew what it was. He'd long forgotten the incident that had remained so vivid in my head. As we had been forced to move out, we were all put on the council housing list. Uncle Graham was the first to get a house for himself and his children; it wouldn't have been practical or possible for us all to remain living together. As we were still waiting for the council to find us a home when the time came for Uncle Graham to move, we had to spend several days and nights sleeping on the floor of the lounge with nothing but a cushion and a blanket. In the empty pub, now closed to the public, with bare rooms and Uncle Graham and my cousins gone, it was strange, spooky and a little sad. I hadn't been happy there, but it was the end of an era and I sensed that whatever was about to come wasn't going to be any better; I wasn't going home, so how could it be?

Eventually we were given a house on a nearby estate, notorious for being rough, but a home nevertheless. A tiny part of me harboured the hope that maybe, just maybe, the change would be for the better and that we might have a life similar to the one I'd known before, now that we wouldn't be surrounded by drunks and alcohol and given that Andy was with us. However, that illusion was shattered when the day came to go and look at our new home. The estate was dark, dirty and sprawling, with cars jacked up on bricks or burned out; there were dogs running around freely, barking at everyone they came across, children who were barely toddlers playing in the street, often slap bang in the middle of the road so that cars either had to go carefully around them or toot their horns until someone moved them ... in the middle of this was our house. A mountain of rubbish and old furniture that had yet to be moved sat in the small front garden and it was a dismal sight.

The inside of the house was not much better than the outside. The thing I remember most was the stale dirty smell and the wallpaper in the living room. It was a dark muddy-brown colour with huge mustard-coloured circles going across it, though not quite circles as each one had a slice cut from it – more like massive Pac-men all over the wall. We had the most basic of furniture, no TV or anything else. Luckily, as I already had a love of books, I spent nearly all the time I wasn't at school reading. I would bury myself in a book, night after night, and try to forget my dismal surroundings.

We saw little of Uncle Graham after this. As quickly as our lives had been forced together, they parted. We did visit a couple of times after he'd first moved, but it soon petered out and I don't remember him ever coming to our house apart from once, years later. Uncle Phil however, continued to come round and abuse me. He would sit next to me on the sofa, a newspaper, cushion or coat strategically placed over our laps, and assault me in the usual way, by inserting his fingers into my vagina; which, by now, was continuously sore.

One weekend, not long after we'd moved in, I was in the kitchen with my mum when she casually mentioned that Uncle Phil would be coming as usual. I took a deep breath.

'I don't like him coming here,' I said. 'I hate sitting next to him because he puts his hands under there.' With that, I indicated my private area.

'Don't be so fucking silly,' she sneered at me.

'Really, Mum,' I went on, 'I don't like it.'

'Stop being a fucking princess,' she said, and walked out, as she always did, stopping any further comments or conversation.

The next day, just as I'd feared, Uncle Phil did arrive and told me to sit next to him almost as soon as he got there. I looked at Mum, pleading with my eyes for her help. She looked away quickly.

'Don't fucking start, just sit down,' she snapped.

With little choice, I did, and was abused in the usual way, while she refused to look in my direction. I have no answers, just questions. All I know is that I did bring it up, I did say, and she just shot me down in the usual way. I just wanted to be back home, with Dad watching the wrestling on the TV, shouting for Big Daddy and Giant Haystacks to win and waiting for us all to go to bed so that he could watch *Tales of the Unexpected*. Mum had started to say that Dad didn't want us; that he didn't want to spend his money on the petrol driving over, but I knew she rewrote history whenever it suited her. When we had gone back, on the trip before she told us we were at the new place for ever, I remember one moment when I started crying. I was so glad to be back with Dad but upset that we had ever been away. A song came on the radio – Styx, I think – and Mum walked in to see me weeping. She said that I must be missing the pub and not to worry as we'd be back there soon. I think she was testing the waters on that trip, seeing how much Dad would let her away with, but what stuck in my mind was how she could take my emotions and turn them into something that played into her version of how she wanted everything to be.

Now, there with Uncle Phil, I wondered if she was doing that again. Was she telling herself that I liked it? Was she telling herself that it was a great reflection on her as a mother if she had an eight-year-old being abused? How could she? I knew what Phil wanted, that was obvious, but Mum? She always acted as if we were all such a burden, and as if she had been miserable for years. She had been married at sixteen, I knew that was true, because Dad had often told me about how she had walked past the garage where he worked as a mechanic and he was smitten with her from the start. I had thought there was love there, I really had. She'd been so different at home, before all of this, before Graham and Phil. She hadn't even been one to swear so much back then; I only really remember her kicking off like that when Dad went looking for her at the pub. Now every second word out of her mouth was nasty. She sexualised everything – you could be talking about the price of apples and she'd sexualise it. It was all normalised for her, so was that how she viewed the abuse as well? Normal?

Any time I made a comment or tried to raise things about Uncle Phil with her, the response would be the same:'Go to your room! Shut up or I'll split your fucking lip!'

I knew one thing – I would never have kids if this was what being a mum was like. I didn't really discuss any of it with Michelle. She spent a lot of time with Mandy and I was worried that I would bother her if I spoke about Phil – would she even believe me? I did wonder if she had seen how he was around me, though. Even if he came in for a 'normal' kiss, he'd be quivering. He always looked like he would spontaneously combust when he was around me, as if it was just all too much; how could no one else see that? He would hang on to me, even when he didn't have his hands up my skirt, shaking, and I knew that he was always getting some sort of sexual gratification from it. I guess other people just thought he was weird, even when he was quivering and dribbling.

It had obviously been Uncle Graham keeping us fed and watered at the pub, as there had always been food available and a meal in the evening. Now food was severely limited; the cupboards were always bare, and we'd go for days with hardly anything. It wasn't unusual for there not to be so much as a crumb in the cupboards, not even a slice of bread, and eventually it became fairly routine. The beginning of the week would be better, when Mum collected her benefits, as she would buy things in and we'd eat fairly well; by the middle of the week things would be getting low, as nothing would be replaced or stocked up until the following week, unless it could be got 'on tick' from the mobile shop that used to come to the estate every night.

After we became regular customers and Mum had successfully managed to flirt with the ageing owner, Ronnie, she soon started to send us for various things.

'Ask Ronnie for this and tell him to put it on my tab.'

Ronnie just used to sigh and roll his eyes at first but as it continued over the years, becoming more frequent and the tab growing longer, he would repeatedly turn me away, leaving me cringing with embarrassment in front of the long queue behind me. Basic things like toilet paper were always in short supply – we had newspaper more than we had loo roll – and if Ronnie refused our request for potatoes or bread, we would sometimes go without dinner altogether. Desperately hungry, I would count the hours until the next school dinner, which I would wolf down so that I could be first with my hand up for seconds. My appetite became a source of amusement to the dinner ladies, who would ask where I put it all.

Mum often shopped at a store called Weigh & Save, a discount food shop in the town centre where everything was stored in huge drums on the floor. It was full of dried goods like cereal, dried mashed potato and stuffing. You would pull a bag off the roll, fill it with a scoop and then be charged by the weight of it. We would often have tubs of dried soup or gravy lurking at the back of the cupboard. None of it tasted very good, but hunger usually got the better of me by the end of the week and I'd eat several bowls of stuffing in the evening to try to fill myself up, try to stop the aching hunger pangs. Friday nights were great though, as Andy would get paid. Knowing the state of things at home, he would bring a 'chippy' dinner. I would fall upon it like a vulture and looked forward to it every week. It must have cost him a lot to buy for all of us on the small training allowance he was paid, but he always did and also gave Mum board money into the bargain.

She was always asking for handouts on top of all this support that he shouldn't have been expected to give in the first place. He was only a sixteen-year-old lad, embarking on his first job. He shouldn't have had a care in the world, but instead he was made man of the house and expected to support his younger sisters as well as his mother whenever she asked it of him. He can't have had any money left for himself and I can only wonder whether, at times, he wondered whether he'd done the right thing by joining us.

While food was nearly always in short supply, Mum never did without fags or booze. Even at a young age I could sense the injustice of this and would be irritated as I watched her puff away while my stomach rumbled for even a slice of bread. She would empty her purse, scouring the house for any coppers or bits of loose change, helping herself to any money in Andy's room, until she had enough to get her next packet of fags. She always managed it, often walking miles to get the cheapest packet. Somehow, though, she never found these resources and survival instincts when it came to feeding her children.

Our estate had a reputation for being rough, so our move to the new house certainly hadn't improved my social standing at school. I spent much of my time alone, while others sniggered at me for my clothes, shoes and anything else they could think of. The move had given me a few weeks' respite from Uncle Phil, but all too soon the old routine was back. He came practically every week now, and with less coming and going as had been normal in the pub, the periods of abuse grew longer. I would be forced to sit next to him, imprisoned by his grip for hours on end, during which time I would read my books, trying to switch off from what was happening to other parts of my body.

Periodically he would whisper, 'Do you like that, is it nice?' into my ear, but I'd carry on reading, not even looking up; if I didn't acknowledge it, it wasn't happening. He also started taking Michelle and me horse riding, first just Michelle, then later, me too. I loved riding and it gave me a love of horses that has stayed with me to this day. It came at a price though – everything did.

On one occasion when he took me by myself, a group of us had been for a ride, and we were back in the tack room where we'd all sit and eat our packed lunches Most of the girls were older than me; I was around nine or ten at the time, and they would have been aged between fourteen and sixteen. As Phil bent down to get something from his rucksack on the floor, his trousers gaped to show the crack of his buttocks. Giggling, one of the girls playfully picked up a riding crop and tickled his bare skin at the bottom of his back while the other girls looked on, laughing. While still bent down, Phil got a handful of straw off the floor, then turned and shoved it down the girl's top. The girl started shouting, but all the while Phil's hand stayed down her top, groping her and laughing.

When Phil went off outside, the girl was in tears and visibly shaken and her friends all gathered round to comfort her, calling him a dirty bastard. They didn't show any hostility toward me, they just seemed to feel sorry for me. I can't see why he was even in there with us to begin with – well, I can, but he shouldn't have been – however, the fact that he didn't seem to be able to control himself was odd. Did he just assume everyone would be like me, that they would say nothing? What if one of the other girls had reported him or told her parents? I don't know if they ever did – I certainly didn't hear anything – but he seemed oblivious to the fact that it might even be a possibility. If that was the case, if he thought he would get away with sexually assaulting a child he didn't know, in public, with witnesses, what chance did I have?

Mum's behaviour was still something I could barely understand. She wasn't the vivacious barmaid she had been in the pub; she didn't even bother to really put that front on any more. We lived in a shithole and she didn't have access to the men or the life of the pub any more – there were different men, that's true, but she wasn't the centre of attention for two shifts every day, and it was obvious she missed that.

She had become friendly with a young hippy lad in his late twenties, who lived nearby. Rob started spending time at our house, or Mum would go to his. He lived about six houses down with his girlfriend but would always come to our place on his own. They would sit there, all over each other, looking at pornographic magazines that would be openly left out on the floor, and sharing roll-ups. Not regular cigarettes, but what Mum called 'wacky baccy'. After smoking these, she'd start acting like she did when she was drunk; they'd be kissing and groping each other all over the sofa or the floor while I tried not to look. If I got upset she'd say, 'Fuck off upstairs if you don't like it.' As their behaviour got more sexual I would disappear to lie on my bed and read yet another book to try to forget what was happening.

Rob seemed to be there when I got home from school most days, and they always found it hilarious to show me their magazines with the most awful images.

'Have a fucking look – you might learn something!' Mum would cackle as she and Rob pawed at each other. I'd run to my room in tears, hearing them grunt and groan in the living room.

There was another man who was there a lot, too. He was much older than Mum and had a wife who was deaf and dumb and I found him really creepy, as he seemed to stare at me whenever I was there, which annoyed Mum a lot.

It seemed as if it was all around me – pornography, sex, grown-ups either ignoring me or giving me the sort of attention I hated. The fact that it was all so normalised added to my sense that I needed to just shut up about what Uncle Phil was doing to me. This was normal. This was what happened. This was growing up.

CHAPTER 5

Princess

ONE DAY, WHEN I was around ten years old, Michelle went on a horse-riding jaunt with Uncle Phil but she came back alone unexpectedly. She was really upset, and I was sent to our room to stay out of the way. I strained to hear what was being said but couldn't make anything out except for Michelle crying and Mum whispering. Eventually Michelle came upstairs and lay on her bed opposite mine, still sobbing.

'What's wrong?' I asked, but she told me to leave her alone.

When I questioned Mum, she told me that Michelle was 'being fucking silly' and that from now on it would be just me going with Uncle Phil. It never occurred to my young brain that he might have done anything sexual to Michelle, even though he had by now been abusing me for over a year. The worst thing I could have imagined happening was that he had hit her, and I thought this is what must have happened. Considering that scenario, I certainly didn't want to go anywhere with him, but Mum said, 'You're not being asked, you're being told.'

I got upset on several occasions before the following weekend, when he was due to take me out, scared of whatever secret event had taken place to cause Michelle to come back so upset, but was told in no uncertain terms to stop being a drama queen and that I'd be going at the weekend no matter what.

I really didn't want to be alone with him any more than I had to, but I wanted to go to the stables and obviously Mum wouldn't let me refuse anyway. I tried to get out of it a few times before the day arrived, but to no avail.

'You're going fucking riding with Phil,' she snapped.

'I don't want to . . .' I'd begin.

'Like I fucking care,' she'd reply. 'You're going and that's that.'

Around the same time, as I waited for the riding weekend to come, I reached another milestone. In the past, I'd frequently be sent to the shops to ask for 'girls' things', as Mum put it. Michelle was in her teens and too embarrassed to buy tampons for herself. You might think that with four sisters and a mother I'd have known a little bit about such matters, but I didn't. Removed from the older ones at a young age, Michelle and I rarely talked other than to bicker and Mum thought that the extent of the maternal role was to give birth.

So, at ten years old I got up one morning and went to the toilet. After wiping myself, I was horrified to find blood on the tissue. Calling to Mum, totally embarrassed, I said, 'I'm bleeding from down below!'

'What the fuck do you expect at your age?' she replied.

I didn't know what she was talking about, but when she said that I'd have to use Michelle's 'girls' things' I put two and two together. Ever the avid reader, I sat studying the leaflet inside the tampon box. I tried inserting one after following the instructions, but it hurt, and I wasn't comfortable touching myself in that area. I was always sore and tender down there and this made it worse. After reading about the risk of toxic shock syndrome I was convinced that if I used one I'd die within hours, so, as I wasn't quite ready for this yet, I folded up a load of toilet roll and used it as a pad. It wasn't very effective, and I had to keep changing it.

Later that night, after I'd used up all the tissue in the house, Mum went mad at me, saying she wasn't made of money, so in the absence of more tissue I used squares of newspaper, which were extremely uncomfortable and even less effective. Eventually I dug out one of my old T-shirts and cut it up and used that instead. I did this for months until eventually I started saving any money I'd find lying around the house, or the pocket money that Andy would sometimes give me, and bought sanitary towels for myself, wearing the same one for days until it was leaking down my legs to try to make them last.

Mum had made it perfectly clear that she wasn't willing to spend money on such things and my reluctance to use tampons like Michelle was yet another example of me thinking I was a 'princess' and 'someone special'.

The following weekend arrived and, despite my protestations, I was made to go out with Uncle Phil. He took me horse riding, which was uneventful in that he didn't try to touch me when we were there, then afterwards we went to his house. I'd never been before. It was a terraced property, the sort with the front door opening on to the pavement. It was dark inside, the curtains were closed and there was barely any furniture, just huge beanbags and furry rugs in the living room, which was separated from the kitchen by the stairs.

In the corner of the room was a long, standing mirror. Uncle Phil told me to look into it as he switched the lights on. Confused, I did as I was told. The lights that came on weren't the overhead lights, as I had expected, but some strange disco lights, which I now know to be UV, the sort you'd find on a sunbed. I remember looking in that mirror and looking at my dark skin, dazzling white eyes and teeth, which all combined to make a very strange effect. The atmosphere was eerie as he sat there watching me look in the mirror.

Uncle Phil took me through to the kitchen and, after passing me a can of Coke from a cupboard (a real treat, having a whole can, and real cola, not cheap stuff!) and giving me some chocolate, he told me to look into the tank that he had in the kitchen. I had noticed it but thought that it was an empty fish tank. It wasn't. It actually housed a huge python that was called Kinky, of all things. I sat transfixed and listened in fascination and horror as he told me how snakes shed their skin and how he bought mice and gerbils for it to eat.

Going back into the lounge with my can, I sat on a beanbag and Uncle Phil lay on the floor on the furry rug. He unzipped his trousers and put one of his hands down inside the front of them and told me to come and lie on top of him. I didn't answer him, look at him or go to lie on top of him. I just stared at the floor and finished drinking my Coke. After lying there fidgeting and grunting for a while he eventually got up, fastened his zip and took me home. Nothing was said, but when I ran up to my room and he stayed downstairs to chat with Mum, I did wonder if they were talking about it.

Well into that night, I was still lying on my bed and crying, for a reason I didn't really know. I was confused and just felt that I didn't want to be me any more and, as always, wanted my dad and brothers and sisters. Mum stuck her head around the door at one point, saw me crying, rolled her eyes and disappeared after muttering something under her breath. I didn't complain again about going with Uncle Phil, as I had a feeling that some corner had been turned. He had taken another step, by doing 'that' in front of me, and I knew there would be no maternal sympathy, never mind action, if I said anything.

From this point, I was going to Uncle Phil's house as well as him coming to ours – and I never got over finding it a horrific place. Like Phil himself, it was just so creepy and weird. He had that snake in one corner of the kitchen, and a Great Dane that he was very fond of wandering around. I would get chills just looking at Phil, with his long white hair and odd clothes. I tried to never make eye contact but I knew that he stared at me constantly, as if he was mesmerised. To this day, I can see him lying on that manky beanbag, slumped on it, with one hand behind his head and the other down his pants, playing with himself and grinning. It was always quite dark as he had such dreary lighting and the curtains were permanently closed, but I would keep getting glimpses of him as he stared at me and worked away at himself. He always had that tin of chocolates on the shelf, too, what I thought of as 'Christmas' chocolates, ones like Quality Street, and he would give me one just before we left, as if it was my reward for 'letting' him touch me or being there while he masturbated.

Afterwards, he would, without fail, take me home on the bus and come in for a few hours, although I always went straight up to my room. I was really far too young to understand any of this. Was this what went on with all mums and all uncles? I didn't know what was normal and what wasn't, and there was no one I could ask. There was no contact with Dad by this point, as Mum had told me he didn't want to see us and had burned all my things (another lie), and I really didn't know whether it was something that was perfectly okay anyway.

I was made to go out with Uncle Phil on a weekly basis. He wasn't abusing me at home as much since the incident with Michelle, but he still took me out, regular as ever, come rain or shine. The horse riding had got less (and it had been the only part that I ever looked forward to) and, more often than not, we would just go to the park and then go back to his house, something that Mum never questioned.

On one occasion at his house, I was sitting on a beanbag while he was sitting on the floor staring at me. He started stroking my feet, then my leg, working his way up from the bottom to the top. He put his hand into my knickers and inserted his fingers into my vagina, forcing me to move my legs open so they were further apart. This had happened plenty of times before, but this was the first occasion when I had looked him in the face while it was happening. He stared right into my eyes, smiling and quivering. I could see saliva on his lips and thought I would throw up. I couldn't speak for fear of being sick or crying and because he was manoeuvring his hand between my legs with more and more force, I slipped off the beanbag and fell backwards onto the floor.

Scrambling up, I ran into the dark kitchen and crouched down in between the snake's tank and a cupboard. I was terrified of what he was going to do next. I just remember staring at the dirty lino on the floor and smelling mould and, damp. Suddenly, I could see his bare feet in front of me and, as I looked up, saw that he was completely naked. I was frantic and honestly thought he was going to kill me. It was the first time I'd ever seen a man completely naked except in Mum's magazines. I couldn't imagine anything worse now that he was stood there like that with his penis sticking out in front of him. I genuinely thought that all he could do to me now was kill me. That was all that was left.

Then, as I was crouched there crying, with my hands covering my face and eyes, it occurred to me that maybe this was what had happened to Michelle. Had he tried to kill her, but she'd got away? If that was true, then why had Mum allowed me to go with him? Why had she insisted? All of these thoughts were swirling round my mind and all the while, for what seemed like hours, I stayed crouched in that dirty corner, the backs of my legs hurting from being bent so long, too terrified to move.

Eventually I heard movement coming from the living room next door and, when I dared to peer around the snake's tank, Uncle Phil came walking into the kitchen fully clothed as he had been before. I hadn't realised that he wasn't in front of me any more; I had just stayed cowering down, waiting for him to do whatever he had planned.

He passed me a can of Coke, acting as if nothing had happened, and told me it was time to go home. I remember wanting to go to the toilet to be sick but being too scared to go in case he changed his mind about taking me home and followed me in and cornered me in the small bathroom. We left without him saying another word.

As soon as my mum opened the door I burst into tears and ran past her up to the safety of my bedroom. In the background I heard her say, 'What the fuck's up with Princess now?' but, though I stayed up in my room all night sobbing on my bed, never once did she come upstairs to see me, either to establish what was wrong or to try to comfort me. This just emphasised to me that what was happening must in some way be normal and that it was me who had the problem. I had never felt more alone. I can still remember that feeling to this day.

I was so very unhappy. When child abuse is compounded by the child thinking it's normal, it really feels like there is nowhere to go. So many abusers, and those who collude with them, push the notion that this happens all the time, that people just don't talk about it, that it is nothing to make a fuss about, that children end up truly not knowing what is right or wrong. They then can't make sense of the awful feelings they have in their hearts and their heads that this *is* wrong. Every message that is given to them suggests otherwise – I had Phil acting as if he could just do it whenever he wanted, Mum telling me I was a fucking princess if I raised my discomfort – so where can they go, what can they do? They are powerless and there seems to be no way out.

It wasn't as if the rest of my life was a fairy tale. At the age of ten, I was becoming very self-conscious and unhappy with my appearance. Unlike most girls of my age, I didn't have the female guidance that I needed to establish my identity. While most girls were starting to have their hair done and going on shopping trips for clothes, I wasn't even guided in the basics of hygiene. I was left to my own devices when it came to washing and only did so when I could actually see something that needed washing off. I never brushed my teeth or was told the necessity of it by my mum. It was the same story with my hair; indeed, all the things that are usually taken for granted as a part of parenting were absent. It was only when I noticed the changes in the girls around me that it actually occurred to me to try to look more presentable. I eventually started trying to wash my hair as often as possible, something that wasn't straightforward, as there was seldom any hot water and I had to bend over the kitchen sink rinsing my hair in ice-cold water, which gave me a headache. I didn't have nice clothes to put on and wearing hand-me-downs was normal to me. The clothes I did own were seldom clean and I would have to drag things out of the laundry pile where they could have been festering for months on end, trying desperately to sponge off any visible stains just to find anything to wear, before returning them to the broken plastic laundry basket housed halfway up the stairs with a mountain of dirty clothes spewing out of it destined never to be washed.

One day, when I was around eleven, I was at Uncle Phil's house. I guess, by that point, I was really just waiting to be abused every time I went round. It was my normality. The curtains were drawn as always, and the strange coloured lights were on. I was sitting on one of the beanbags in the living room when he came over and gave me a can of Coke. This was unusual, as he generally handed me one as a treat after he had abused me.

I was looking at slides of horses when he came over and knelt in front of me.

His trousers were pulled down around his thighs.

His penis was exposed.

I looked away, but he raised the upper half of his body, putting his penis at my eye level, and pressed his pubic hair against my cheek.

I was horrified.

'Lick it,' he said.

I sat, shaking, thinking that if I didn't look he wouldn't make me do it. Not that, surely not that. It was disgusting, *he* was disgusting, and he smelled so very much.

I should have known.

Holding his penis, he got hold of the back of my neck with one hand and started to push my head down towards it.

'Go on, lick it, you'll like it.'

He always said that.

You'll like it.

Do you like it?

I bet you like that!

Words that chill me to this day.

I tried to pull away but he had tight hold of my hair and continued to force my head down. I clamped my mouth firmly shut, which meant I had to breathe through my nose. The sour stench of urine and everything else connected with him made vomit rise in my throat. I don't remember it stopping or anything else, only the sensation of feeling sick and dizzy and my head hurting from my hair being pulled.

I think I must have dissociated.

In that house of his, I always felt that he wanted to kill me. I thought that was why he had me there. The acts he was doing, the things he was forcing me into, were so appalling that I thought he would go further, that he wouldn't know when to stop. I think I did have a sense that he had no boundaries. I was often focused on what he would do next, whether on that visit or visits to come, and I feel that I was just in survival mode.

Princess

This time he'll do it, I often said to myself. *This time he'll kill me.*

I knew I couldn't discuss it with anyone. I knew no one would save me. It felt like there was a big secret that everyone was a part of and that I was the only one who found it unacceptable. It all seemed fine with Mum so far – if Uncle Phil killed me, would that be fine too? Maybe she'd be glad to see the back of me, maybe she'd cover for him, maybe I would be one less thing to make her life a misery. The only thing he could do that was worse than what he was doing already – I had thought – was to take my life from me. And I thought that everyone would probably be fine with that. After all, no one had fought hard to get me back.

I'd been told that Dad didn't want me, that my other siblings were glad that I was out of their lives, that my possessions had been dumped or burned. I couldn't tell Andy – Andy loved Uncle Phil. He wasn't the type to judge people on their appearances, and was something of an outsider himself. It would never have entered his head that there was anything amiss. Mum would have wriggled out of it, she would have said I was a liar, a fucking nightmare, that nothing ever pleased me and that Phil had always done his best.

I really did feel that no one would believe me, and no one would think it mattered. Everyone always asks survivors, why didn't you tell? Why didn't you get out of it? But *who* do you tell, *how* do you get out of it? I want people to stop asking that question because it's nothing more than victim-blaming dressed up as concern. The truth is, I wouldn't even have known how to articulate it. It happens, it had happened, but I didn't know what *it* was if I had to describe *it* to someone else.

Abuse goes on and it gets bigger and dirtier. It gets more and more shameful, and the victim feels that the shame lies with them. As you get older, you feel people can see it on you, sense it on, smell it on you. The abuser copes – it is what they want, they are getting exactly what they hoped for – but the child? They carry it.

If I could take anything from that time in my life and build something from it, something good, something pure, it would be this: never assume that you know the life of a child. Never assume that they are acting out because they are 'naturally' naughty. Never assume that they are quiet because it's just their nature. Never assume that because they are hungry it's because they are greedy. Never assume that they are dirty and unwashed because they defy their parents' calls for them to have a bath or change their clothes. Never assume anything. Paedophiles hide so much and so well, but so do their victims. At the start, before they even know what it is, maybe that's when they might tell – I don't know for sure, because it never applied to me; I never told back then. But, as they get older, as they become part of it themselves, as they are groomed to believe that people will look down on them, that no one cares, that no one will listen, then they hide things too. They hide the shame and the disgust they feel about themselves. They start to think that they have let themselves down, that the younger version of them should have spoken up.

That they've missed their chance.

That they've missed their chance to get out of it.

Shut up.

Don't say a word.

Fucking princess.

How would I get past all of that? How?

CHAPTER 6

Family

DURING OUR FIRST year at the house, Mum had a few boyfriends; not as many as she'd had at the pub but a few nevertheless – she added some more to Rob the Hippy, and the creepy old guy, and also picked up again with a skinny Italian man who she'd been seeing while we lived with Uncle Graham. She would often tell me details of her sexual exploits, and details about the physical nature of the men she slept with, and I would get very embarrassed and uncomfortable – I have to admit, though, that I was also quite pleased that Mum was talking to me as if I was a grown-up. It was only when my own daughter reached the same age that the inappropriateness of this fully hit home; the thought of having such a sexually explicit conversation with her at that age was repulsive and it made me start to realise how wrong my mum's behaviour had been. It was only in later life that the total lack of parenting in my childhood hit home. I felt worthless when I realised. Why was she never concerned at my distress? Why did she swear at me all the time and allow me to witness things that I should have been protected from? And why had she never thought that I was anyone special? I *should* have been special to her, surely, even if not to anyone else.

One day, in my final year of primary school, Mum told me that we were going to visit her older sister, who lived not far from us. I couldn't remember ever having met her before and Mum had only mentioned her occasionally. All I knew was that she was called Thelma and that she was older than Mum.

I remember the bus journey, walking to Thelma's house and being met at the door by a large smiling woman who embraced me as if she had known me and loved me all her life. I felt so comfortable with her immediately, and the fact that she made me huge portions of food as soon as I walked in the door was the way to my heart. Mum seemed to get on well with her, which was surprising to me, and after dinner they sat and talked about things I didn't understand while I listened in.

Some time later, my cousins arrived home. I watched, amazed, as they bounded in, happy to be home, helping themselves to snacks and hugging their mum. I felt pangs of envy at how happy they looked and the lifestyle they seemed to have. Not the material things, but the laughter and affection that they all shared, which obviously came naturally to them. It seemed a lifetime since I'd had anything like the same, had my brothers and sisters around me. I really did long to have it back.

Just as it was getting dark and was nearly time for us to go, a man arrived. He turned out to be Auntie Thelma's husband, my Uncle John. He'd just cycled home from work and he sat in his chair while my cousin Robert, who was a little older than me, sat on his lap and Auntie Thelma brought him tea. They seemed like a really happy family and I was envious at what they seemed to have.

As we left to get the bus home, Auntie Thelma hugged me tight. She smelled of soap and cooking and felt so safe. I could have cuddled her for ever. Mum kissed her goodbye, then went to kiss Uncle John. They kissed on the lips for what seemed like quite a long time. I looked around, feeling a bit uncomfortable, but nobody else seemed to be taking any notice so I quickly forgot about it and made the bus journey home with her.

My outings with Uncle Phil were never-ending at this time, or at least that's how it felt. The horse riding had long since stopped and there was no longer any pretence that I was going anywhere other than to his house or to walk his dog with him. This dog, the huge Great Dane called Frip, could put his feet on my shoulders when stood on his back legs and he just added to the general odd air of his master.

I would be made to go on these walks whatever the weather. If I tried to object or make excuses, Mum would go off on one and often refuse to speak to me for a couple of days, so it was a whole lot easier just to go and get it done with. On one occasion, it was winter and there was a lot of snow. Uncle Phil and I had gone to walk the dog on what were locally known as 'The Chads', a large area of hilly common that sprawled for about a mile, leading to a park and boating lake. I remember wearing wellies and Uncle Phil rolling a huge snowball down the hill while I held onto Frip's lead. Eventually the cold and the snow made me need the toilet. I kept hanging on and hanging on until I couldn't hold it any longer. Home was about a ten-minute walk away, which seemed too far when I was desperate for a wee. Uncle Phil told me I would have to go behind a tree. I didn't really have any option, so I hurried over to the most secluded tree I could find and pulled my pants down around my knees while I crouched down low to do my business. A moment later, while I was mid-flow, I felt something slip under my bottom between my legs. Disgustingly, Uncle Phil's hand, wet from my pee, stroked my private parts. I was so shocked and embarrassed; I quickly got up, pulling my pants up with me. We kept walking, with Uncle Phil throwing snowballs and making snowmen as if nothing had happened, as was always the case, leaving me confused and thinking that maybe in some way it was either normal or my own fault.

Mum and I had been to see Auntie Thelma a couple of times. In fact, sometimes she would tell me that she had been while I was at school. One day, when I came home, I saw a pushbike in the kitchen. Curious, I looked through the door, thinking we had a visitor and trying to guess who I knew with a bike, but I saw no one.

'Hello!' I shouted but was met with silence.

I went upstairs to see where Mum was.

As I reached the landing I could hear grunting noises. Mum's bedroom door was slightly open, and I wondered if she was maybe poorly. Just as I went to walk in, I saw Uncle John and her, both naked in bed with him on top of her and everything in full view. Shocked, I just stood there, not knowing what to do or say, until Mum turned her head and caught my eye.

Smiling, she said, 'Aren't you going to say hello to your Uncle John?'

It was as if they were sat having tea and cakes. I was so confused. I wanted to cry. I moved to go downstairs, away from the vile sight that was in front of me, but as I left she shouted, 'Shut the fucking door after you next time.'

Downstairs I sat crying, confused and angry, thinking about Auntie Thelma and listening to the sound of the bed creaking. The groans from above made me want to rip my ears off. In the end I turned the telly up as loud as I could to try to drown out the noise. Much later they both appeared downstairs, and Mum made him a cup of tea before kissing him at the door in her dressing gown as he left. Afterwards, she went about her business as usual, as if nothing out of the ordinary had happened. She sat smoking for the rest of the evening, sometimes staring at me, smirking, as if waiting for me to catch her eye, almost willing me to say something. What could I say?

This became a regular occurrence. Several times a week I would come home from school to find her and Uncle John in bed, with no effort made to cover anything up or restrict their activities to when the house was empty. There was even less food in the house than usual as it seemed Mum was always in bed having sex or smoking. Time after time I would arrive home and my heart would sink on seeing Uncle John's bike propped up in the kitchen, and then I'd hear the rhythmic squeaking of the bed and frequent moans and groans coming from upstairs.

One time I arrived home and she was nowhere to be seen, but as John's bike wasn't in the kitchen I assumed she must be having a lie-down. I knocked on her door and went in, only to find her under a heap of covers with Uncle John's watch on the floor beside the bed. I asked her if he had been and she smirked and said, 'He's still here.' She pulled back the bedcovers in dramatic fashion as if to reveal a prize, revealing a naked Uncle John with his head between her legs. Starting to cry, I asked her what he was doing, and she said he was looking for his watch. I walked away with the sound of her sneering laughter in my ears.

I was around eleven years old by this point and getting ready to go to high school. I still had very few friends and, to be honest, I could see why – I didn't really have much to offer apart from my company and even that can't have been too interesting a prospect. I was so often miserable and emotional for reasons I didn't understand, so I definitely couldn't explain to anyone else. I think that my emotions were all coming to a head, and I was flooded with hormones anyway, as well as longing for the life I had once had. On top of that, I was being regularly abused and subjected to Mum's constant sexual exploits. I had my books and I had my imagination, but that was pretty much it. In my imagination, I had lots of friends, I was popular and I never went hungry. I would go from happy schoolgirl to mature woman in my dreams. I had a career (there would be no children for me), a handsome boyfriend who worshipped me and never wanted anything more than a cuddle, and a lovely house of my own that I wasn't ashamed to bring my many friends to. These sessions of fantasising became more and more frequent and I promised myself that one day, when I was old enough to get away and do something about it, it would all become a reality.

When I had started my periods, I had hoped that once Uncle Phil realised, it would be an end to the ritual of him inserting his fingers into me while everyone sat around. But it didn't stop him at all. He would arrange things in the usual way and, hidden by newspapers or coats, would pull whatever padding I was using as a makeshift sanitary towel to the side and carry on as before. When he would remove his hands, I'd be able to see the blood under his fingernails. I'd feel embarrassed and sick, especially when he made no effort to hide it or go and wash his hands, but would just wipe them on his trousers or jacket. He was filthy at the best of times, but this made it even worse.

As I got that little bit older I would increasingly take myself out of Phil's way and appear to be really busy doing homework or tidying my bedroom, something that Mum couldn't berate me for, which in turn meant that the abuse became that little bit less frequent. I got a surge of satisfaction and accomplishment when he would visit and leave without being able to put his hands on me, but I was still forced to go out with him if Mum decided that she wanted the house to herself.

On one occasion, when she had sent me away with him, I remember him lying flat on the floor with some music on in the background. He was wearing lilac corduroy trousers and, as the song finished, he told me to go and choose something else to put on. As I stepped over him to look through the records, he reached up and grabbed on to my arm, pulling me down so that I fell onto his pelvic area. He was pressing on my back to draw me closer to him, so I put my hands on the floor at either side of his head, trying to push away so that my face wouldn't be near his and trying to stop him from making me lie on top of him. I was wearing a skirt and could feel something hard and sticky on the inside of my thigh.

Looking down, I could see his erect penis against my leg. He pulled my knickers to the side with one hand and pushed hard on the bottom of my back to force me down closer over his penis. I could feel the coarseness of his pubic hair against me and as he jiggled his hips around I felt a pain I'd never experienced the like of before. A stabbing, tearing pain that went from my private parts all the way up to my stomach, leaving me sick and breathless.

Wriggling and crying out in agony, I managed to roll off him on to the floor. He stayed there on the floor propped up on his elbows, his penis still erect and exposed, making no attempt to try to cover up but just looking at me a bit sheepishly.

While I didn't fully understand what had just happened, we both knew that this time he had gone further than ever before, and I didn't know how much more I could take. I felt dirty and worthless and couldn't see any reason to carry on living. My private parts were throbbing, so I hurried upstairs to the toilet to hide and clean myself up.

When I came back down, my face swollen from crying, he handed me a can of Coke, slipped his coat on and opened the door, indicating that it was time to go.

Uncle Phil chatted away on the bus as he always did, as if we had just had a lovely day out. Mum didn't question my tearstained face or the fact that I ran straight upstairs. I ripped a small rectangle of mirror out of a jewellery box and tried to look at my vaginal area, expecting to look as bruised and disfigured as I felt, as I was in agony. I saw nothing, but I also had nothing to compare it to as I had never looked at myself intimately before. I did, however, see Mum looking through the gap in my slightly open door, watching me. When I caught her peeping, she walked away without saying a word. The soreness lasted for days and when I passed water on the toilet the stinging pain would take my breath away, leaving me crying until it passed.

Uncle John was still a frequent visitor and spent more and more time at our house, sometimes all day. At other times he would turn up saying he only had an hour. When they didn't rush straight to the bedroom to make the most of the time they had, they would occasionally sit downstairs, and I actually got to know him a little bit. He wasn't the sort of person that I was used to. He was a quietly spoken balding man with a southern accent, really normal, completely unremarkable – not the sort of person that you would expect to be having an affair with his wife's sister.

Family

The affair continued for what seemed like a very long time, though in reality it was probably only a matter of months. Throughout my last summer at primary school there was rarely an occasion that I arrived home and they weren't in bed together. All that greeted me was the smell of smoke and sex and the screeching of the bedsprings from the ceiling. If I dared to go up and ask if there was anything I could have to eat, or make my presence felt in any way, I would get a mouthful of abuse.

'Does it fucking look like it?' she would spit, making no attempt to cover anything that was on show. 'Do I look like I'm about you make you a fucking meal? Put your fucking face straight.'

Michelle and Andy both had social lives by this time, so I spent long periods alone in the evenings when they were out. Uncle John would make unannounced visits, apparently on a trip to the shops, as far as my auntie believed. How he explained his hours of absence for those shopping trips, I don't know. He would make random appearances, much to Mum's delight, and they would immediately disappear upstairs, where the squeaking and moaning would go on until he hurried off back into the night on his bike, back to his wife and children, my auntie and cousins.

Ironically, the little attention and company I did have really only came from Uncle Phil, as his visits continued, though now he was increasingly choosing to stay at our house to abuse me, rather than take me to his. I'm guessing he must have realised, as I got older and after my crying out on the last occasion, that it was easier to get away with what he was doing in our house. I was less likely to create a fuss, knowing the reaction I would get.

One evening, as I was about to go to bed, there was a knock at the door. Mum answered and Uncle John walked in with his pushbike. It was later than was usual for his visits and I heard her ask him how long he could stay for.

'For ever,' he replied.

Hearing that and seeing our inquisitive faces as Michelle and I hovered around, Mum sent us immediately up to bed and banned us from coming down.

That night, as we lay in our beds, Michelle and I talked and tried to imagine what it would be like to live with a man in the house. Despite Mum's many male interests we'd never had a man other than our dad and brothers actually living with us. We knew it would make her happy but didn't really think of the impact it would have on everyone else, including Auntie Thelma.

Any romantic notion that we were going to transform into a modern-day (but completely dysfunctional) Brady Bunch was quickly dispelled. Uncle John moved in that night and, from that point on, Mum's life revolved around him 24/7. When they weren't in bed, they sat in the lounge smoking. If we sat in the lounge ourselves we felt in the way, as if we were intruding on their time. We weren't included in any conversation, and if I interrupted their bubble by asking a question I'd be brushed off. It was easier to spend the evenings in my bedroom reading, until the inevitable time when they decided to go to bed. The moaning and groaning would start up, and I'd go to sleep with the radio on to drown out the noise.

Life at school was still unpredictable. Sometimes I would be able to tag along with a certain group of girls for a few days, or even weeks, and I'd start to think that I had a chance of fitting in. Then, out of the blue, the same girls would blank me and walk away when I went to join them. They'd huddle in a corner, making it obvious that they were talking about me and laughing. I never knew where I stood so it was easier to keep myself to myself and not give them the satisfaction of making a fool of me. My school reports would often say that I preferred to work alone on projects rather than with others. The teachers never questioned why, so I continued to withdraw inside myself as a defence mechanism.

Primary school was coming to an end and, after the summer, I'd be going to the same Catholic high school that Michelle attended, along with most of the others from my school. I was terrified at the prospect but at the same time I think a tiny part of my ever-optimistic subconscious hoped that maybe things would slot into place for me. I knew I'd meet hundreds of new people and, while it scared me, it also gave me hope that amongst them I might at last find a true friend. Someone who would like me for who I was and not make fun of me or turn their back on me. I craved a friend. I had no one in the world to talk to or confide in and I carried around a constant loneliness.

I don't remember much about the holidays except for trying to get out of the house as much as possible. Mum and Uncle John continued their relentless noisy sex sessions at all hours of the day and night. They always left the doors open for all to see when we walked past and started taking baths together with the door open. They made friends with our new next-door neighbours, people they could drink and smoke with all day and night. The air was like smog and my throat was sore from breathing it in. They had started home-brewing beer and wine as a cheap way to get drunk. The beer was kept in the airing cupboard in my bedroom while it fermented or whatever was supposed to happen. The smell was horrendous; the strong bitter stench of yeast filled my tiny room, making me feel nauseous all the time. Naturally, when I dared raise an objection I only got a mouthful of abuse.

My life was bleak, but I don't think it was unique in many ways. Children who are abused often have nothing else to hold on to: there is no parent who loves them, so, in a twisted turn of fate, they only have the attentions of their abuser. Uncle Phil never threatened me. Even when I thought he was going to kill me, it wasn't because of anything he said, it was because that seemed the next logical step for me (in a mind that couldn't really process this logically) and because I couldn't really work out what was happening. I loved Thelma, but I knew there was something very odd going on there. Michelle and Andy were much older than me – something bad had happened between my sister and Phil, I sensed that, but Andy adored him. I had no school friends and I was in a toxic family set-up that was being portrayed as completely normal. What on earth could any eleven-year-old do in the middle of that?

CHAPTER 7

UNCLE PHIL CONTINUED to come round once John moved in, but less often. He rarely took me to his house any more, but still sat in the lounge and would continue to abuse me if the opportunity arose. This was becoming less frequent now that Mum had a man in her life to occupy her. Whereas before she would have forced me to sit next to him, now it moved on to her telling him to ignore me.

'Let her get on with it, she thinks she's a princess and her shit doesn't stink,' she'd say.

Up until now, despite everything, I'd actually loved her a lot. Children often love their parents unconditionally whether that love is abused or not. I still loved Mum, but around this time I started to vehemently dislike her.

Most of this came from frustration and an increasing awareness that her behaviour was not as acceptable as she'd have me believe. I would get wound up to the point of bursting at the way she spoke to me. If I did something she didn't like or went a bit out of line, instead of telling me off or grounding me like other parents would have done, she'd say horrible things.

'I'll split your fucking head with a brick if you carry on.'

'Stop being such a precious little bitch.'

'I gave up fucking years for you, you have no fucking idea.'

At this age and already feeling that the whole world was against me, I would just look at her in disgust. I even started to answer back, asking her why she had to say such nasty things. This would usually result in me getting a slap around the face, but I just couldn't hold in my resentment at times.

We still had very little food – there was more than before due to John bringing money into the house, as he had a job with a refrigeration company – but we'd still run out of even the basics for days on end until payday, whereas they would empty their wallets and purses and turn the house upside down, then walk miles in order to get hold of the cheapest packet of fags they could.

I didn't see much of Pete or of my other sisters. They would come and visit sometimes but Mum would either make out that everything was hunky-dory or that I was turning into a horrible moody teenager who she couldn't please for want of trying. Which angle she went for would depend on if my most recent behaviour suited her or not.

Over that summer, Mum and John started going for hikes. Occasionally she would ask if I wanted to go with them; with little else to do and glad to be included for a change, I went a few times. I was happy to be away from the estate and get a bit of fresh air and it wasn't unenjoyable, but I stopped going because, whenever we reached the top of any hill, Mum and John would strip down to their underwear, with her going topless, in order to cool down and 'be at one with nature'. I found this mortifying – we weren't up Kilimanjaro and it was totally unnecessary, just more attention-seeking.

As the return to school got ever closer, I got more and more anxious. The only saving grace for me was that I wouldn't be totally alone as Michelle would be there. Going into her final year, she had promised to show me around and help me if I got lost. We weren't exceptionally close at this point. I was sad, confused and had no life outside of our house, whereas she had boyfriends, friends and the usual sort of social life that a girl of that age has. I was just her annoying little sister. We did have some fun sometimes though. As we shared a bedroom, we would mess about and put make-up on each other and, having a similar sense of humour, we would laugh for hours. We spent a lot of time recording ourselves singing, convinced we were going to become famous pop stars if we ever sent our tape to a record company!

Towards the end of the holidays, Mum had started knitting. She was quite good at it and often made cardigans and bootees for the babies in the family. This time she said she was making me a school jumper, as she couldn't afford to buy one. The uniform I was supposed to wear consisted of black skirt, black shoes and a pale-blue round-neck jumper that everyone bought from the same uniform shop in the town centre.

We hadn't been out to get any of it so far as she had been so wrapped up in Uncle John. I presumed she would just be leaving it to the last minute, as we did with most things. When she said that she was knitting me a jumper I felt a bit apprehensive, especially when I saw the picture on the front of the pattern and it didn't look anything like the one that Michelle wore. All I wanted was to look the same as everybody else and I was panic-stricken at the thought that I might stand out. I reasoned that the wool must have cost money so I didn't understand why we couldn't have just gone and bought a proper one. Mum made it clear that the matter wasn't up for discussion and the knitting continued.

The jumper was finished the day before I was due to start and I stood with a heavy heart while she slipped it over my head and admired it.

'What do you think?' she asked.

I didn't know what to say. I felt very ungrateful after the work she had put into it and it was nice to have a mum who had done something for me for once. The jumper itself was okay; it just didn't resemble the school one we were supposed to wear. I also knew it would make her angry and hurt her feelings if I said how I felt, so I said that I was really pleased with it and the fancy pattern she had put on it and tried to hope that maybe people wouldn't notice, and things wouldn't be so bad.

Any hopes I had of fitting in faded fast when, on completion of the jumper, Mum went hunting around the house and came back with an old skirt of Michelle's that had never been worn because it was out of fashion even when it was bought. She also brought in a pair of brown boys' shoes that had been acquired at some point, which were several sizes too small. The skirt was a wide A-line one that was too big around my middle and had to be rolled over on the waistband in order to stay up, but when I tried to protest that I couldn't possibly wear it, Mum growled that it was that or nothing. As with the skirt, I was made to put the shoes on, but they were really tight. My toes were curled up at the ends and even walking across the room was painful.

Nearly in tears, I begged her to think of something else. She raised her eyebrows at me and I knew that I was never going to get my way.

'They're the wrong colour too,' I said, in a last-ditch attempt to persuade her. She disappeared and came back with a tub of black shoe polish, then proceeded to scrub the brown shoes until they were completely black.

'Now what have you got to fucking moan about?' she said, throwing them at my feet.

That was me ready for my first day at high school.

The next morning, while Michelle got ready and was looking forward to seeing her friends again, I pulled on my huge skirt, knitted jumper and dirty grey socks that had been white many generations ago. Cramming my feet into the tiny shoes, I looked at the end result in the mirror and felt like crying. I was scruffy and humiliated and my feet were already in agony – and I had a twenty-minute walk ahead of me.

Michelle met up with some of her friends on the way and, as my shoes were rubbing so much, I soon started lagging behind them. Along the way we kept passing other new starters, walking with friends, excitedly sharing the anticipation. Michelle was true to her word that morning and stayed with me while she caught up with all her friends, though I generally just followed her around and hung behind her. She made sure I was okay though and, every time they moved on, she always checked I was following. The worst thing was seeing all the other girls in their sparkling new uniforms with fashionable shoes and smart new bags. Most of them had trendy new hairdos to boot and were all comparing their things. Desperate to see a positive side, I remember thinking that I wasn't going to miss the girls from my old school anyway, and, as I could see a few girls wandering around by themselves, I dared to hope that maybe I would make a whole new group of friends.

Any fantasy I harboured of a new start, of being liked and accepted, very quickly went out of the window; I found high school to be even harsher than primary. This period was one of the toughest of my life, and that's saying something. Michelle soon got bored with her younger sister trailing around after her. She wanted to swear and talk about boys like every other fifteen-year-old was doing at the time, without worrying that I might repeat something she wanted kept private, so it wasn't long before she started doing her own thing and I was left to wander around by myself.

The girls (and in fact the boys) seemed to be grouped into categories. There were the 'geeks' – the kids who were all really clever and in the top sets. While smartly dressed, they weren't interested in being trendy or popular; they just wanted to do well at school. They had their own close-knit circle of friends that they could depend upon and earned a certain amount of respect for doing their own thing and being clever.

Then there were the 'populars' – the attractive and trendy ones who wore the coolest clothes and always had a posse of people laughing at their jokes. They were in demand; everyone wanted to be in their group. They seemed to sail through school without a care in the world.

Next, there were the 'loners' – the ones who wandered about by themselves, trying very hard to look as though they didn't care. They weren't in this category by choice but because they didn't 'fit': their faces, clothes or circumstances weren't conventional enough to be worthy of people wanting to get to know them. Treated as the butt of people's jokes or worse, ignored altogether, neither exceptionally clever nor attractive, we were the nothing kids who existed day to day and counted down the minutes until we would be away from the dreaded place. Even the teachers seemed to favour the clever and attractive ones and seldom seemed to make the same effort with the 'nothings'.

I was a fully fledged member of the 'loners' and, looking back, I can see now that we were a group of kids with our own individual range of problems. No one could have guessed mine, nor I theirs; we just needed someone to see us for what we were and not what we weren't. I guess that some of the kids in the other groups had their own problems, too – I know now that what other people see you as isn't necessarily the truth of your life; however, back then, I longed to be anyone but me.

The following few months passed in a blur. The nightmare of high school was interspersed with visits from Uncle Phil, when the abuse continued as it had always done whenever he got the opportunity. His visits had dwindled, though, and since the incident where he'd hurt me he seemed warier. By this time, I was going through puberty and developing quite quickly. I was no longer a little girl and was starting to look like a fully fledged teenager; even though I was only eleven or twelve, I was often mistaken for fifteen or sixteen.

Life at home and at school was something I endured. I was only really happy when I had an occasional visit from my brothers and sisters or when reading books. I was picked on for my clothes all the time and, on top of this, as my thick dark hair had become quite greasy, I earned the nickname 'Crisp 'n' Dry.' It came from an advert for cooking oil and groups of boys would start singing it whenever they saw me or sat near me in class. Horrified, I would wash my hair as often as I could, usually with washing-up liquid and freezing cold water, as that was generally all we had, but it never stopped the torment. I felt ugly and worthless and dreaded walking past them knowing what was coming.

One day, as I was walking to school, I just felt that I couldn't take it any more. Home was bad enough and school was the icing on the cake. I couldn't subject myself to any more misery. I just stopped in my tracks, turned around and walked to the far side of the cemetery that lay behind me, where I sat on a bench reading the headstones for hours. It wasn't planned; I just couldn't bring myself to keep putting one foot in front of the other in the direction of school. As time ticked away I realised that I couldn't really sit there all day and, after a moment's thought, started walking in the opposite direction to home.

As I walked down the side roads out of view I realised I was in spitting distance of Auntie Doris. Not a real auntie, she was an elderly lady who used to clean the pub when we lived there. We had visited her a few times after moving but hadn't seen her in a while, and she and Mum never crossed paths now that Uncle John was on the scene. I went to call on her and she was really pleased to see me. She didn't get out much and was obviously lonely and glad of the company. When she asked about school, I told her that the teachers were on strike and she didn't question me any further, despite me being in my uniform. She sent me to the sandwich shop for pies and cream cakes for our lunch and we sat talking until it was time for me to go. I was glad to have missed school but convinced that my secret would be out once I got home. It turned out, though, that I had got away with it, so I continued to truant and visit Auntie Doris for over a month.

When Doris asked me anything about school I would let my imagination run riot and invent the sort of school life that I longed for. I told her about my close friends and the things we'd got up to and that they all wanted to invite me for tea. I hadn't given any thought to how long I could continue without being found out; we weren't on the phone back then, so I didn't have to worry about school calling. I was just enjoying not having to endure daily misery.

I arrived home one evening to Mum, who had a

strange look on her face and asked me how school had been. I came out with the usual rubbish, whereby she told me that an Education Officer had been round and told her that I hadn't been to school for weeks. She was understandably angry, screaming and crying about all the lies I'd told her. I told her where I'd been going but never once did she ask why I'd skipped school in the first place. Not once. She was just angry that I'd made her look bad.

The next day, the Deputy Head came to speak to me with Mum there. He sat on our sofa telling me how I'd let my poor mother down, while she put on a hangdog face as if she was bereaved. He didn't ask me why I'd done it, either. It was all put down to yet another case of me being moody and rebellious. I looked at my mother sitting there while the teacher insisted that I reflect on the pain I had caused her! I hated her with every ounce of my being that day and ached for a mum who would take me in her arms, tell me everything would be okay and bother to ask why I was so blatantly unhappy.

When I went back to school, a couple of the teachers' kids who'd been to my primary school had been assigned to keep me company in an obvious attempt at preventing a recurrence, though the whys and wherefores had never been discussed. Even the other kids didn't ask where I'd been. There were whispers that maybe my mother had died, but I grudgingly told them this wasn't true, as the last thing I wanted was their sympathy. They didn't ask any more questions and obligingly let me follow them around for the next few weeks until they were no longer forced to accommodate me; the bullying, fuelled by my mysterious absence, continued, though a little less fiercely. Still I desperately wanted out of it all, though, in one way or another.

As I hurtled into my teens, while my circumstances may have remained the same, my mindset grew increasingly angry and self-hating. I was angry for everything that had happened, continued to happen and the life that I was living. I didn't need compliments, I just needed to feel that I was a likeable person who was worthy of being loved. I grew thick skin and, whereas once I used to take myself off when confronted with verbal abuse, now I would front it out and sit there, determined not to give anyone the satisfaction of knowing they'd hurt me. Alone in my bedroom at night, I would practise looking in the mirror and smiling, even though I felt sad and miserable. Strange behaviour, I suppose, but it was my way of reassuring myself that if I could smile in the face of everything then I would survive.

As far as school was concerned, there was a slight improvement, in that I wouldn't be alone as often as I used to be. I would tag on to different groups of girls, as and when they allowed. Even though I was on the outside looking in, it still gave the impression that I was included, and, on those occasions it got me through the day. As this was only sometimes the case, I had an enormous amount of absence from school. I would constantly claim to be ill in the mornings; often I would be so anxious at the thought of school that I would go to any lengths to avoid it. I had got into the habit of going to sleep with the radio on to try to drown out the sex noises from the bedroom next door, though it never did. Ironically, if the radio was above a murmur, Mum would throw a shoe or something at the wall and tell me to turn it down, then carry on puffing and panting with John.

The radio also acted as an alarm, so I would set it for 6 a.m. with the intention of making vomiting noises in the toilet, then going in to Mum to tell her I was ill. Unfortunately, I often didn't drift off to sleep until 3 or 4 a.m. due to their sound effects, so would frequently sleep right through the alarm and wake with a sickening panic when I realised I wouldn't have time to try to convince her that I was unwell. I still managed to miss a lot of school though, as Mum often couldn't be bothered with the effort of trying to make me go. It usually didn't take more than her putting her head around the door to tell me to get up and me saying I didn't feel well for her to storm off, slamming the door behind her and saying, 'What a fucking surprise.' Even when I was at school I'd dodge the lessons that were hardest for me, not because of the subject, but because of who would be in the class and the torment I'd get. On these occasions, I'd hide in the toilets until the bell went for the next lesson.

My attendance at school began to improve when Mum worked out how to get clothing grants. These were vouchers that were only accepted at certain shops, but it was a vast improvement and meant that I never again suffered the humiliation of that first year. Still, somehow, I never got it right.

The girls at school always had their own code of fashion and what was currently acceptable, so every year I would buy the style that they had been wearing only to find that, when we returned to school after the summer, they'd moved on to a different style. I was always a year behind.

Obviously, my academic achievement was affected by my situation; apart from my massive number of ongoing absences, when I did attend school I found it next to impossible to concentrate. I was constantly nervous and on edge, and very self-conscious about being the subject of any teasing or of the other girls' discussions. There were even a couple of teachers who made life particularly hard for me. One was the woodwork teacher, a man who always smelled of cigarettes. I didn't particularly enjoy the lesson, none of the girls did, but he seemed to have an intense dislike for me personally. He would regularly make derogatory comments towards me while paying the other girls compliments in an almost flirtatious manner.

One day he made the whole class laugh when I entered the classroom a couple of minutes late. He sang,

'Katie, Katie, where is your father now?' to the tune of 'Daisy, Daisy.' While a couple of kids were a bit shocked that he had said it, the majority of them thought it was hysterical and spent the rest of the lesson laughing and singing it back to me.

The other teacher who seemed to really not like me at all was the sociology teacher. This was one of my favourite subjects, so I tried to get on with my work and keep my head down, but she would always instigate a confrontation with me. If I so much as asked to go to the toilet, she would make a big issue out of it, but she'd let others go. If I put my hand up to ask a question, she would shout at me and make it seem as though I hadn't been listening. She'd sit me next to my male equivalent (a boy who was always poorly dressed and had no friends), then make everyone laugh by saying what a nice couple we made. She'd comment on the other girls, saying that they looked pretty or whatever, then look at me and say that there wasn't much you could do with some people. I can honestly say that woman single-handedly made me feel worthless and ugly for years. What she got out of doing it I will never know.

My school reports generally said that while I was capable of achieving, I didn't apply myself sufficiently. The next few years up, until I was around fourteen and began to gain a little independence and control over my life, were a blur really. A miserable state of existing without any happiness or purpose other than to plan the life I dreamt of having in the future. I knew now that my circumstances weren't 'normal' but also knew that there was no one for me to turn to. Mum had already painted me as a rebellious, moody teenager to anyone who would listen, and I knew how she'd twist things if I tried to tell anyone the way things really were. I'd heard her do it a million times.

Any hopes that being with Uncle John might mellow her soon disintegrated. If anything he orchestrated situations for her to be angry with me and encouraged her to be spiteful. Besides the open sex they continued to have in the house, John used to lie on the bed with the door wide open when Mum wasn't in the room, masturbating. He was in full view when I would walk past, which was often, as I had to go past their bedroom on the way downstairs. All in all, I constantly felt on edge and uncomfortable and would have done anything to get out of that house.

Even my summer holidays were spoiled. I usually spent several weeks of them staying with one of my sisters, but Mum and John started to come along, too. Once, when staying with Debbie – who was now married with two children – we shared a bedroom with one double and a single bed pushed next to each other. It was practically like having one huge bed and it certainly didn't stop them. So close that we were practically touching, they continued to have sex alongside me until I turned to face the wall and cry quietly.

This wasn't good enough for Mum, who flailed her arm over to smack me in the face.

'What the fuck's up with you now?' she shouted. 'Stop fucking snivelling.'

Uncle Phil still came fairly regularly to abuse me. Uncle John had his weird ways and would constantly be nasty or encourage Mum to be, as if she needed any encouragement. School was the same, though I eventually made a couple of casual friends who I drifted between until we all left. The frustrating thing for me was that my mum would portray the situation in an entirely different light to my brothers and sisters – no one else ever saw her behave the way she really was. As time passed, nothing changed, and I got through by reading in my bedroom and planning my future life.

When I was fourteen, I started a Saturday job at the local Wimpy bar. With my £10 wages, as well as food, I'd buy bits of make-up or clothes off the market and experiment in my room until I got quite good at it. I decided that when I left school I'd study make-up at college. My appearance improved as I had more control over it and I began to get some attention from boys when I went out. They would whistle or get their friends to come over and ask me out. I was flattered by the attention but didn't want a boyfriend, so always refused. This was in stark contrast to school where, in my uniform and without make-up, the boys still teased or ignored me. I certainly wasn't girlfriend material to any of them.

I also saw my dad again during this time for the first time since I was eight years old. He was getting remarried and my brothers and sisters all said he wanted me there. Facilitated by them, I saw him on the morning before his wedding, when he hugged me tightly and said how much he had missed me. I was so happy to see him and it was like the years in between had all melted away. I hadn't met his wife before but she was lovely and clearly adored my dad, which was enough for me.

'Incidents' with Uncle Phil were becoming less frequent by this point. He certainly visited less. In hindsight, I was probably getting too old to appeal to him as I definitely looked like a young woman by now. On one of his visits when I was fourteen, I felt him staring at me. I was wearing electric blue skin-tight silk trousers that I'd got from a jumble sale, what they call disco pants now, and he couldn't keep his eyes off me. I was pudgy with puppy fat and he was openly lecherous, licking his lips and gawping at me. Ignoring him, I sat down on a separate sofa, but he came to sit next to me. Mum was embroiled with John and couldn't care less. My feet were up next to me and he began stroking them, always the prelude to any abuse. I got up to move away and he grabbed my wrist tightly, trying to pull me to sit back down, staring me straight in the eyes as if to warn me. Returning his gaze, I snatched my wrist away from his grasp with Mum looking on.

Out

'Leave me alone,' I said, clearly.

'Don't fucking start, don't fucking say a word about wanting to be left alone. This is what she's like now,' ranted Mum. 'This is what I have to put up with.'

Turning away, I went to my bedroom feeling exhilarated that I'd stopped him from touching me. I knew somehow that something had changed. It was a feeling, a sense that there had been a shift in the power balance between us. I didn't think my body was really what he wanted any longer. He was touching me out of habit now rather than for his perversions. Mum's complaints about me, too, were often just like background noise, I had listened to her for so long. In my room, alone, I looked at myself in the mirror and thought, *This is different. That, that thing that happened there – whatever it was, whatever strength you found to walk away – that was a sign. He won't touch you again, Katie.*

I was right. I wouldn't even see Uncle Phil for another twenty years after that night. I was out of that. Out.

PART TWO

CHAPTER 8

This is What You Are

WITH UNCLE PHIL and his sexual abuse of me a thing of the past, my confidence started to soar as I began to believe that maybe I was capable of controlling my own destiny. I spent increasing amounts of time out of the house, going for long walks or just wandering the streets to avoid being at home when Mum and John were there. I had no respect for him whatsoever. He'd never made any effort to be friendly to me and he certainly wasn't my father. After a lifetime of being told what to do, I'd had enough and was starting, in my own way, to rebel. Obviously this caused even more confrontation, but I was beginning to get satisfaction in standing up for myself and no longer cared if they blanked me or were nasty. It was nothing new and over the years I'd been forced to grow a thick skin. There was no longer much more they could do to hurt me.

Something else happened when I was fourteen that seemed to me the most normal, but also the most unlikely, thing in the world – I got my first boyfriend.

Our family had started to have bottles of fizzy pop delivered from a lorry every couple of weeks. Whenever I went to pay, the young delivery boy would always chat me up. He came to my house twice on 'dates' but really just sat on his motorbike outside or on the sofa holding my hand until it was time for him to go. Each time, I went outside to say goodbye but never wanted the inevitable kiss. I liked the idea of having a boyfriend but didn't want the reality of one. I was seemingly self-assured and had built a convincing mask of confidence, but when it came to anyone trying to get close I backed off. It was attention and affection that I was looking for and nothing else. Needless to say, most boys wanted more than to hold hands, even if it was just a goodnight kiss.

Michelle was pregnant by this point. Whereas I hated the idea of having children and wanted a career and to travel the world, she had always loved babies and had wanted a baby for as long as I could remember, so she wasn't unhappy when she came home one day and told us the news. She had been casually seeing a lad at the factory where she worked, and though at the time it was nothing serious, she was delighted. After one particularly nasty row with Mum where Michelle told her that she'd make a better job of bringing up her baby than Mum ever did with us, she was told to pack her bags. I did miss her, even though we had argued a lot.

One time, just after the fizzy drinks boy had dumped me, Mum asked if I wanted to come along to the local working men's club while she worked on the bar for the night. In a good mood for a change, I jumped at the chance, still ever-grateful of her positive attention. She supplied me with soft drinks while I sat in a corner watching the customers drinking and a group of men playing darts.

One of the men kept looking over at me and smiling. Flattered by the attention, and being completely confused by boundaries, I shyly smiled back and he came to sit on the seat next to me.

'I can't concentrate with you there,' he said, smirking at me. 'What's your name? What age are you?'

I told him, but he didn't believe I was only fourteen and went to the bar to ask Mum about me as she already knew him from previous visits to the club. She laughingly confirmed my age and commented that all the girls in our family were 'well developed' and that I was 'mature' for my age, clearly encouraging him to pursue me. He kept saying to her, 'I'm completely distracted by your daughter!' and she was absolutely buzzing with the deflected compliments. She acted as if she had achieved something.

While this man Barry was obviously older than me,

I hadn't realised he was actually twenty-eight and was recently separated with a couple of children – a fact my mum was well aware of. He asked me out and, with encouragement from Mum, I agreed to meet him a few days later. I wasn't particularly attracted to him but was flattered by the attention and thought it would be very grown up. Most mothers would be mortified at the prospect of such a man showing their young daughter attention in that way and forbid it. Mine was positively beaming and acted as though it was a positive reflection on her; she even made a comment about me having got my looks and charm from her.

We had agreed to meet at a pub that I'd never been to and, with my mask of confidence in place, I walked in. Seeing that he wasn't there, I got myself a drink and sat at a table near the door where I could easily be seen. Barry looked almost surprised to see me when he finally turned up. After getting himself a drink, one of the first things he said to me was, 'So how old are you really?'

'I've already told you – I'm fourteen.'

'Jesus, I thought you were joking,' he muttered, shaking his head and swearing under his breath. There was an awkward silence for a minute before he seemed to make a decision; we started talking again and the moment passed. During the course of the night, the half pint of cider that I'd got for myself was swiftly followed by several shots of straight vodka that Barry insisted I have. Needless to say, I was soon very drunk – and I loved the feeling. It made me forget everything else and I sat there in a contented haze. That first taste of vodka was the start of me using alcohol as a crutch to forget the past – and the present – in years to come.

Having had little experience with boys up to that point, I had no comparison or frame of reference as to what was or wasn't acceptable or how I should feel. Most teenagers get guidance and support from their parents, family and friends during these years; I had none of this. With no real friends and most of my family miles away, the only message I got was from Mum, and it was that any attention from a man was better than none. If you didn't enjoy the attention, then that was because you thought you were better than other people and above yourself: a strange message to pass on to your young daughters.

So I thought nothing of my lack of anticipation or excitement at seeing Barry, or of my distaste when he kissed me goodnight. I didn't know how I was supposed to feel. After our first date, Mum said I was 'glowing'. Presumably this was the effects of the large amounts of alcohol. I was so lacking in any awareness of what was right or appropriate in a relationship between a 28-year-old man and a fourteen-year-old abused girl that I didn't even hear any alarm bells ringing when, one night I turned down the offer of dancing with him and he exploded and started shouting and swearing at me in front of everyone. He said that he knew he'd made a mistake going out with someone so young and that unless I grew up he would dump me. Inexplicably concerned at this thought (and at the prospect of no longer being plied with alcohol), I agreed to start being more agreeable to whatever he wanted.

'Well, you can start by spending the night with me,' he stated. He was still separated from his wife and children and was now sharing a house with his mother.

Miserably, I nodded in acceptance.

'In future, if I say shit – you shit!' he told me, charmingly.

It seems unimaginable now that I ever accepted that sort of treatment, but that is looking back as an older, reasonably strong woman who knows what she does and doesn't want. At the time I was a lost fourteen-year-old who was very uncomfortable in her own skin and just wanted to be wanted, by anyone.

Mum – appallingly – agreed to me spending the night with Barry and, as the date grew closer, I began to worry that he might expect me to sleep with him, despite my age. When I met him at the pub, he already had several drinks lined up for me and said that as he had been drinking for a while I had to catch up. Desperate to prove my maturity, I downed the various shots. This binge-drinking continued for several hours until, much earlier than we would have usually ended the evening, he said it was time for us to go back to his house.

The minute we got in he checked that his mother was in bed. Then he proceeded to get us more drinks from the kitchen. I was feeling really sick by now and all I wanted to do was sleep.

'Well, you're not fucking well falling asleep on me,' he told me, pulling me down on the sofa next to him. Before I could speak he was all over me, kissing me so hard that I could hardly breathe and pulling at my clothes, pushing his hands under my top. As he slobbered all over me, his hands became more and more insistent. I was repulsed and started to panic. Visions of Uncle Phil were flashing through my mind while this man twice my age, who I barely liked, let alone wanted to be intimate with, mauled me. Catching my breath, I pushed him off as hard as I could, moving his hands from my body.

Taken aback, he sat up abruptly and looked at me, his face red with anger.

'What's the fucking problem?' he whispered angrily, clearly trying to keep his voice down so as not to wake his mother.

'I just don't want to,' I told him.

'You are fucking joking!' he replied. 'You've been leading me on since we met. You know what you are? Do you? Do you know what you are? A little fucking tease. I warned you not to say "no" to me, I fucking warned you. Get out. Just fucking get out.'

'I can't! I've got no way of getting home – I don't even know where I am. Honestly, Barry, it's late, there won't be any buses.'

He sighed. 'Okay. Okay.' The relief flooded over me.

'I'll give you one last chance. You going to sleep with me, or not?'

'No, no I'm not,' I confirmed.

After calling me a load of unsavoury names, he went upstairs, slamming the door after him. I sat there on the sofa wondering what to do. This was before mobile phones were commonplace and there was no one I could have called anyway. Eventually, drunk and exhausted, I no longer cared and just lay down to get the sleep that I craved.

The next morning, I was woken by Barry shoving me roughly and telling me to get up as he had to leave for work and would drop me off on the way. He was clearly still angry, and we sat in his van in silence. When we reached my house, he stated that he wouldn't be seeing me again, in case I was in any doubt, and pushed me out of the van, slamming the door after me. Tired, hungover and fed up, I sat on the back doorstep trying to clear my head.

Moments later, Mum opened the door behind me and yelled at me to come inside the house. I started crying, not over Barry but I think because my only possible route to escaping from home had now disappeared. Exhausted from lack of sleep, I crawled into bed, completely bewildered by Mum rushing around telling me that she was hiding all the sharp objects in the room, and to remember that there were plenty more men out there. I suppose she was trying to be supportive in her own way, but the idea that she thought I was suicidal over a man was quite funny really.

Over the next few years my independence began to grow as I realised that the only way to keep my sanity was to spend as much time out of the house as possible. After the Wimpy burger bar in the town centre, I moved on to a new part-time job on a clothes stall in the famous Ashton market. I used to get £10 for a full day's work, which meant setting up at 8.30 a.m. and standing in freezing weather until after 5 p.m. I actually really enjoyed meeting people and loved having a bit of money. I had a couple of boyfriends during this period, but they were nothing serious and I was determined that I would be different from Mum. My world would never revolve around a man. I had firm plans for my future and was determined to become a beautician. I had no qualifications, so I applied to a college in Stoke. My brother Pete had a flat now and said that I could stay with him for a while if I needed to, and Mum just said, 'It's your life' when I told her. I couldn't wait to start, back near my brothers and sisters and in the place that I still felt was home.

But when I started to make arrangements, and it became clear that my plans were not just a pipedream, Mum's attitude changed. I still had over six months of school left, but whenever I discussed my plans she would become moody and often not speak to me for days. When she did, it was to make comments designed to make me feel guilty, like saying I couldn't wait to get away from her and that I was too busy sorting myself out to care about anyone else. I would usually go to my room when this started, to avoid the atmosphere. When her tactics didn't work, she'd start to be uncharacteristically nice to me, making my favourite dinner and saying, 'You won't get this when you move out; what am I going to do without my little girl to talk to?' I'd hug her and reassure her that I would still come and see her a lot. This only seemed to fuel her resentment and she would push me away, then return to silent mode and not speak to me again for several days. It was draining.

Things reached a head when I had to send the acceptance slip back to the college. I felt terrible and, as much as I disliked her as a person, she was still my mum, and she'd succeeded in making me feel terribly guilty, as though I was abandoning her.

'I'd be as well killing myself!' she announced when she saw the slip. 'I'll have nothing to live for – but you just go on and live your life. Go on!'

I was distraught and screwed up my acceptance letter and told her that I'd stay. I think a small part of me was gratified that she felt strongly enough to want me there, but I didn't really understand why, as we didn't have a good relationship the rest of the time and she still continued to make nasty comments and be sexually explicit in front of me.

With the future I had planned now non-existent, I started to feel very down and was angry with myself for being so weak. I still hated school, so I got a job in a newsagent and never returned to the place that had caused me so much misery. I was fifteen, without a qualification to my name, but I thought I was free.

I loved working and I loved not being at school. I had over £43 a week in wages, so as well as buying clothes and make-up, I could also afford to start going out to bars and clubs. While it was a long time since I'd had any childhood to speak of, I was keen to leave the young 'me' behind and reinvent myself as a grown-up, independent woman. I didn't want marriage and kids, that wasn't who I was – I wanted to be completely self-reliant with as few responsibilities as possible. I'd already learned that you couldn't depend on anyone but yourself.

Over the next few years I did focus on myself. I had no real plans for the future other than to get away from the estate and Mum's mood swings. Her sex sessions were still as indiscreet as ever and I hated every moment that I was in the house. I spent as much time away from there as possible, going into town with Michelle, as we were getting on well by that stage. She had a baby boy whom I adored and spent a lot of time with while she did bar work in the evenings.

We'd buy a bottle of vodka and a bottle of sweet Martini from the off-licence, as cheap as we could get. Michelle would put them in her handbag and then, at the first pub we went to, we'd buy a couple of halves, drink them and keep the glasses. For the rest of the night we would head to the toilets as soon as we went in anywhere and fill our stolen glasses up with the illicit booze. On top of this, there was usually a lad or two willing to buy us drinks. We became experts at having a night out on a budget.

I was never interested in the sexual side of things with men, but I did enjoy being chased and getting attention. After years of no self-esteem, the attention I got from boys when I went out made me feel pretty and as good as everyone else. When I did have a boyfriend, it was only affection that I really wanted, though obviously they always expected more. I had several sexual encounters over this time, a few one-night stands and a few with boyfriends who never lasted longer than a couple of months. The experience never lived up to expectations and I eventually started to think that sex was something that had to be endured in order to sustain a relationship, a sad way to think at the age of just seventeen.

I got a lot of attention from boys but the only ones I ever really took a liking to were always already in a relationship or not interested in me. I didn't know what I wanted from a relationship and probably wasn't even ready for one, hence the few boyfriends I did have would be dumped a couple of months down the line for no other reason than I just couldn't be bothered. I never felt the fireworks that all the books I read said you should feel, so didn't see the point in going through the motions when I was happier being on my own.

I was so young, but I was wishing my life away. All I really wanted was a house of my own, though I didn't know how I was going to achieve this. I was living for the moment, convinced that something would happen to change my life for ever so that my past became a distant memory. Little did I know that this was exactly what was about to happen and that the demon waiting around the corner for me was just as bad as the mostly miserable existence I'd had up to that point. I'd get the attention I craved, but I'd pay a heavy price.

CHAPTER 9

Jump

I'D STARTED SEEING a lad called Neil who worked in one of the bars in the town centre. One afternoon, I went into the bar on my lunch hour from my job at a bus company, planning to meet my sister-in-law Kaye for a few drinks. Neil wasn't there and Kaye and I settled on a sofa to chat for a bit. The place was pretty much empty, as it usually was on weekdays, apart from the same old drunks who would sit at the bar day after day drinking £1 pints until they fell over.

Two men in suits were wandering about and one of them in particular was following me with his eyes. Kaye had noticed and mentioned it. I laughed and joked that small men in suits were not my type. Eventually he came over.

'Are you Neil's girlfriend?' he asked.

'I am,' I confirmed, smiling.

'I'm Martin. His boss. The owner of this place.' He swept his arm around grandly, as if it wasn't a complete dive.

We talked for a few minutes as he paid me some compliments and asked what I was doing with someone like Neil. It was small talk with blatant flirtation on his part. He really was nothing to look at, although he seemed very confident, and I had no interest in him at all, despite his flirting. I thought I should be nice to him as he was Neil's boss but, on the next few occasions I saw him at the bar, he always made a beeline for me and eventually I started talking to him for hours while I waited for Neil to finish work. He told me he was separated with a young baby. I didn't think much about it except that I thought I remembered Neil saying that he was married, not separated.

He went on to ask me about work. I told him I liked my job and earned good money.

Out of the blue, he asked, 'Do you fancy working for me? I've just set up a property company – got a smart office a couple of streets away. I'll be buying more bars soon. And nightclubs. Loads of them.'

'No – you're all right,' I said, thinking it all seemed like pie in the sky, but he quickly said he would pay me a lot more than I was getting at the bus company and offer fantastic career progression. Well . . . this could be just what I needed. More money and promotion could take me closer to getting a house of my own.

'You'd be managing the office, interviewing staff, that sort of thing. You would have lots of responsibilities,' he went on, reeling me in.

I was young and flattered by it all. He was so persistent. Every time I saw him, there were more promises, more temptations. Inevitably, I eventually agreed. I'd no reason to believe Martin was anything other than genuine and it seemed like too good an opportunity to turn down. I left the bus company and started to imagine my new job at the heart of his modern, professional, ambitious empire. I was young and this could be my first step towards amazing things.

I met Martin on the street outside a really old building that seemed quite underwhelming. However, I knew lots of those old buildings were often renovated amazingly inside, so as we walked up the stairs, I was still optimistic.

It didn't last.

We arrived in a space that was really just two rooms linked by a door. It was grotty and tiny, with one filthy window that looked down onto a miserable street below. In the first room (where I would be based) there was just an old-fashioned desk and a chair with some pens and bits of stationery placed next to a telephone. The door from my room led through to the other, much larger office, which was more elaborately furnished, with a leather chesterfield sofa and a glass display cabinet containing champagne, along with an expensive-looking desk. Martin said that this was where he would be working.

The environment was far from what I'd imagined, but I told myself that I could still go places. Unfortunately, there was only one place Martin wanted to go. From the moment I started at the office, he pursued me relentlessly. It was flattering, though exhausting, as I wasn't attracted to him at all. Even though he knew I was with Neil – and was being nice to Neil's face – he continued to make advances all day, every day.

After a few weeks, I became completely disillusioned with my supposed 'step up' the career ladder. From 9 a.m. until 5.30 p.m. I would sit at my desk, literally twiddling my thumbs, waiting for the phone to ring, which it rarely did. Martin waltzed in and out between the bar and the office, but even when he was there it was only to continue his efforts to get me to end things with Neil and be with him. He would buy me presents, usually a watch or jewellery, and when I stayed firm, he would sulk like a little boy who wasn't getting his own way. The truth was, I didn't know what I wanted. I certainly wasn't in love with Neil and only continued to see him because I felt too guilty to tell him how I felt. I had never done this before; usually I just made myself completely unavailable until the boy gave up.

However, Neil had started to talk about us getting a

flat together and was making plans for the future. I was waiting for the right moment to tell him that it wasn't what I wanted. I didn't know at that age that there is never a right time. On the other hand, I also knew I wasn't attracted to Martin in a physical sense, let alone in love with him. I was flattered by his attentions, though, and he was completely different from anyone else I'd ever met before. Though only twenty, he appeared much older, not just because he dressed in suits and had his own business but because he also had a very eccentric way about him. He was extravagant and impulsive, and had a way of making me feel sorry for him without me ever really knowing why. Although it was him who pursued me, he made me feel that by constantly rejecting his advances I was leading him on. At that age, I didn't have the presence of mind to properly evaluate my feelings and act accordingly, otherwise I would never have been with either one of them. I also wasn't equipped to realise when someone was being emotionally manipulative. He would buy me gifts and try to kiss me, then throw the presents across the room when I turned away, leaving me feeling guilty and ungrateful.

Martin did, however, make me laugh, largely down to his strange little ways. It was with an element of resignation and impulsiveness that I eventually caved in after yet another awkward moment in his car when he was dropping me off one day. He lost his temper.

'Everyone thinks we're together anyway,' he said.

'They're all gossiping about all the time we spend together, so you might as well accept that it's going to happen.'

It was always his doing, all the time we spent together, and he just never stopped going on about us being a couple, about sleeping together, so I gave up. I had always hated the physical side of being in a relationship, but I was always so malleable when it came to other people's needs and demands. Despite it not feeling right, and despite the lack of physical attraction on my part, I did think Martin was quite sweet and funny. He seemed to be offering security and the chance to experience things that I'd never had before. He had the business, a nice car, he said he had his own house and he always wanted to take me out to restaurants, the cinema or the theatre. While these wouldn't be remarkable things to most people, I'd had so little life experience – I'd never eaten out or seen a show – so while I wasn't consciously thinking materialistically, my eyes were being opened to a bigger world than I was used to. The chance to experience new things was exciting; the only boys I had previously been out with had always lived at home with parents and I was lucky if they had a job or a pushbike. So, with all this and his relentless pursuit, I thought, 'Why not?'

Never has one careless decision had such an impact on my life. It was a decision that would affect everything and bring me more pain and misery than I'd ever known.

There was Martin, with his promises and his life of possibility. He was persuasive, he said he adored me, he said it would be wonderful. And me? A teenager who had been ripped from her home at such an early age, sexually abused, emotionally abused, psychologically abused – what chance did I have? I wanted a life, I wanted to get away from everything bad, so I took this chance on someone who seemed to have had me in his sights from day one. In later years, I would wonder – was there something about me? Did I have 'VICTIM' tattooed on me? Was there some signal I sent out that meant abusers zoned in on me, knowing that my self-esteem and confidence was so low that they could do pretty much anything they wanted. I wondered, I really did.

As soon as that fatal decision to be with Martin was made, my life changed for ever and started moving at breakneck speed. Now we were officially a couple, it was expected (by him) that all of our time would be spent together. On my seventeenth birthday, just days after our first kiss, Martin took me to Blackpool. I naively thought that we would be returning the same night and was taken aback when, without any consultation, he took me to a B&B that he'd already booked. I know it will sound silly, but the idea of sleeping with him had never even entered my head. I just didn't think of him in that way and was only just getting my head around the idea of us being a couple at all.

As would become par for the course, I was made to

feel that I should be grateful and flattered for anything that he did, and any decision I made or any suggestion I had that things might be different was met with such opposition, sulks and tantrums that it was far easier to go along with what he wanted. With the exception of Mum's emotional blackmail, I'd never experienced such manipulation, so was completely blind to the fact that, from day one of our relationship, this was exactly what was happening on a grand scale. I'd gone straight from the frying pan to the fire, no doubt about it.

For someone who pursued me so aggressively, Martin went to enormous and relentless lengths to try to change me, to mould me into the person that he wanted rather than the person I was. We had very little in common. Martin didn't know my likes or dislikes, my hobbies, ambitions or interests, how I felt about important issues, or what I wanted out of life. In fact, in all the years we were together, he never bothered to find out. He simply wasn't interested. Everything was about how I made him look, and that had to be favourable at all times. We went to the places that he chose, did the things that he wanted, and I was expected to go along with it all without question and be extremely grateful.

I was still living with Mum at this point and just wanted any opportunity to forget the past and be out of the house. Martin would frequently book hotel rooms for us, several times a week. He was still telling me that he was living alone after separating from his wife and baby. I never went to his house – he said it wasn't very nice and that he was looking for somewhere better. I was such a fool.

On a few occasions, I'd spoken to him on the phone while he was at home and had heard voices in the background – even the sound of vacuuming once. When I questioned it, he said that it was the TV, or it was the day for his cleaner. I naively took it all at face value and thought no more about it. It was only months down the line that I discovered he'd still been living with his wife and didn't separate from her until I'd agreed to move in with him and he'd found a flat for us.

The picture he painted was one that is pretty much a script for married men who don't want to get caught or make a commitment until they absolutely have to. He told me they had separate lives and separate beds (don't they always?). He said that this had been going on for a while, that he only stayed with her for the sake of the baby and because she was mentally unstable and she didn't understand him. He really wasn't original at all. However, he felt so strongly for me that those feelings took precedence. The reality was a lot less romantic, and a lot more telling about the type of man Martin was. It had, in fact, come pretty much out of the blue for his wife when he announced that he was leaving. Their baby was only three months old, much younger than I had thought, and here he was parading around with a seventeen-year-old as if he'd won the lottery. She very much thought that I'd taken him from her knowing he was a married man, which wasn't the case at all. At the time however, young and very stupid, I ignored any nagging doubts and accepted his version of events. I was so desperate to get out of the life I had into one that would be the right fit for me that I jumped without looking.

During the first months of our relationship I was given many insights into Martin's character that should have had me running for the hills, but I didn't notice any of them. For a start, he was obsessed with the gangster lifestyle. He had a sidekick, a Scottish man called Pat, who acted as a manager at the bar. Martin hero-worshipped this man, who was as just as manipulative as he was and claimed to have connections with and be a part of the criminal underworld in Glasgow. In reality, Pat was an overweight, unattractive, middle-aged man in a shell-suit with sovereign rings and a completely misplaced sense of his own power. He had a lovely wife, who he treated like dirt, and two young daughters. He was also having an affair with a seventeen-year-old – they had their own little club, really, Martin and Pat.

While it was expected that I would be friends with Pat's lover, Maria, she was similarly expected to behave a certain way and accommodate his every whim. I think this is where Martin learned how to act. He was very enamoured of Pat and influenced heavily by him. He'd had no positive male role models in his life since the death of his grandfather when he was much younger, and I think Pat filled that void. Martin was only three years older than me but seemed so much older that it was easy to miss how impressionable he was. He and Pat both carried imitation guns in holsters, which they justified by saying they needed them as 'protection'; it was almost laughable – no one cared or really even noticed them.

They would go to various 'meetings' in a local pub while Pat's girlfriend and I were made to sit and wait for them in the car outside. It was absolutely forbidden for us to come in with them and when they left us to go to the 'meeting' they would say they'd be back in ten minutes; but it was always actually a couple of hours, which was a long time to be sat in a car twiddling your thumbs. They would eventually waltz back, half-drunk, without so much as an apology. Looking back, I'm not even annoyed at the way I was treated; I'm just angry and amazed at what a complete idiot and mug I was. Even while writing this, I cringe at my own idiocy and wish I could go back to the girl I was and slap some sense into her. But there was no guidance from anywhere and I probably wouldn't have listened anyway. I was angry with the world and desperate to escape from myself and forge the new life that I was foolish enough to think would put the past behind me and be the answer to all my problems.

CHAPTER 10

True Colours

WITHIN WEEKS, MY brainwashing had begun. Martin asked me to move in with him and he found a nice flat in a good area. Any doubts I had were overtaken by my desire to be away from Mum and the house I'd been so unhappy in. She wasn't happy to begin with but, after a few initial protests and some pouting – and also under the impression that Martin had money – she gave up and accepted the inevitable.

In the process of moving out, a significant incident occurred that, in hindsight, should have made me question the whole thing. I'd packed my worldly goods into a huge box that Martin had brought round. The box used to house a TV, so it was huge, easily able to contain my clothes, books and a few sentimental items such as photos and teddies. It was all put in the box, which was then placed in the back of Martin's car. Every night for the next few days, when we arrived back at the flat I would walk round the car meaning to take the box out.

Martin would always say, 'Leave it until tomorrow', and that he couldn't be bothered carrying the massive box up the stairs to the flat. This went on for about a week until, one afternoon while I was at Mum's picking up a few more things, Martin phoned to say that he had some bad news. The box containing all my stuff had been stolen from his car while it was parked outside the bar. On this one occasion he had left the car unlocked, and with the box in clear view on the back seat it was an open invitation for any passing thief to help themselves. It would have taken two people to carry the huge box and its contents, but they had managed it. To add insult to injury, some photobooth pictures of me and a friend that had been in it were found in a corner of the stairs leading up to the bar, meaning that whoever had taken my things had then had the cheek to go back into the bar. I was totally devastated. I'd been looking forward to what I hoped would be a new start, and now it was ruined. There was nothing of value in the box but there was lots of sentimental stuff that my brothers and sisters had bought me and a tiny jewellery box that used to belong to my grandmother, not to mention every item of clothing that I owned.

Looking back, I now see that this was a sign, a huge

marker of what was to come. The disappearance of that box marked the beginning of Martin erasing my entire personality and history. I had nothing left that indicated anything about me as a person or my hobbies or interests, and all my mementoes of good times past were gone, as well as my links to my family. I couldn't have known at the time, but this was the shape of things to come. I would no longer be allowed to have my own thoughts and ideas. I was to be moulded into the person that he wanted me to be.

Martin would spend the next twelve years running me down and trying to ensure there was nothing left of the inner me. My life before him wouldn't even be acknowledged and I would no longer be a person in my own right, only an extension of him.

I didn't realise until over twenty years later that my family all firmly believed that he had disposed of my belongings himself, probably seeing them as unimportant and a nuisance in the back of his car. This had never occurred to me, so deep was I into his world by then, but it certainly made a lot more sense than his version of events.

We moved into the flat and, whatever I'd expected, the reality of the situation certainly didn't live up to it. I'd thought I was taking control of my life, moving away from Mum and the awful memories of my past. I was just desperate for normality.

I was immediately told that I wasn't allowed to give our address to anyone, including my family. Martin's reasoning was that he had run up debts at the bar and committed some kind of fraud that the police would want to question him about, so he had to keep a low profile. It was better that people knew as little as possible, he told me, adding to the gangster persona he was so desperate to cultivate. I did argue the case for my family to know where we lived but he got extremely angry, to the point where he said that maybe he'd made a mistake moving in with me. He was very good at this sort of logic, at backing me into a corner so that he got what he wanted. The deal was always, do what I want or get back to your mum's house. I didn't know how to explain any of this to anyone as I didn't really understand it myself.

Shortly after moving in together, the bar closed and Martin opened a nightclub in the city centre. We led an unconventional life, out all night and asleep through the day. We had no household essentials, no vacuum, no freezer or washing machine, as we were rarely home except to sleep. All our meals were either takeaways or in restaurants. Martin had given no thought to the practicalities of life, as he'd always had someone to take care of everything for him: first his grandma, who had brought him up, then his wife. He only ever wore suits, no matter what the weather or occasion, but soon started complaining when his shirts mounted up. I had no skills in this department at all. I hadn't been taught and hadn't had an example. Suddenly I was expected to cook, clean, wash, without any facilities to do these things. Martin would leave leftover takeaway food on the floor and shout when I didn't move it. He was completely used to getting his own way and having every whim catered for, and if that didn't happen he would explode in anger. We ate what he wanted, where he wanted, when he wanted. Any resistance on my part or desire for anything different was met with arguments and he would manipulate me into thinking that I was being awkward. I told myself that, even though things weren't as I'd hoped, they were still better than life at Mum's had been. I was determined to never go back.

After he closed the bar and opened the nightclub, the office where I 'worked' became a commercial estate agent for a little while, and it was through this that he found his next premises. Although it was more on a back street than in the city centre, he was convinced this would be his shot at the big time. It soon became apparent that this is what he was constantly chasing.

He had delusions that he would become a highly respected millionaire – not a normal or vague wish for a better life, but a narcissistic obsession. Martin was utterly convinced that he was more intelligent than everyone else and destined for a much higher purpose in life. He wanted to be anything but ordinary. He refused to get normal employment as he said that he was too clever to line other people's pockets and he wasn't about to have anyone else tell him what to do. He actually was very clever; he just didn't channel it in the right way. As a child, he'd been singled out as having a high IQ and was offered a free scholarship to a respected boarding school, but turned it down after an initial visit. This information came from his grandma, not him, so I knew it was true. Many of the things he told me when we met and over the coming years turned out to be total fabrication. I think he created versions of events that were easier for him to live with than the actual truth of the matter. For example, he said that he was due to inherit a large sum of money when he was thirty and that this supposed inheritance would come from his late father, who had died when he was a child. It would be such a fortune that it would enable him to retire and live a life of luxury.

That was the root of most of his issues, I think: his paternal heritage, or lack of it. Martin never knew his father and was raised by his grandparents. His mum had become pregnant in the 1960s when she was only fifteen, at a time when it was frowned upon for unmarried girls to fall pregnant out of wedlock, especially at such a young age. Martin's version of events was incredibly romantic but, at first, I had no reason to disbelieve it. He said that his mother had fallen in love with an older married man who was a wealthy, highly respected barrister, living on his own estate with his family. His version varied from time to time in that he sometimes said that this man had never left his wife, while at other times he'd say that he had been born on this estate and his mum had lived with this man for a while. Irrespective of which version he was telling, Martin's father always got knocked down and killed when he was a baby and too young to remember him. He said that he'd been told all of this by a solicitor friend of his father who had always kept an eye on him in order to tell him the truth when he came of age. This was also supposed to be the reason for his mother's ill health. Still young when I met her, she spent all her time reclusively in her house, chain-smoking and falling asleep due to constantly over-medicating herself on prescription drugs.

It was all a bit Dickensian really, and Martin kept adding bits to the story every time he told it. He said that his mum had suffered a breakdown after his father's death, been prescribed antidepressants and had never been the same since. His grandma told me years later that Martin had been born in her front room and that his mum had become pregnant after a one-night stand with a lad of her own age who she had never seen again. Not believing her to be responsible enough to care for a baby, and also to stop tongues wagging, she and Martin's grandfather had agreed to raise the baby themselves. His mum lived in the same house but did nothing for him, they took on all of the responsibility for the baby. I was never quite clear as to whether they had passed Martin off as theirs, but that did happen back then with families who tried to hide 'scandal', so I suppose it might have happened here.

They refused to ever speak about it to Martin, and when he was of an age to start asking questions about his father he was always told flatly that he was dead and to be quiet. This must have been difficult for a small child to hear and was no doubt where his many versions of his heritage came from. He did, however, have a positive role model in his maternal grandfather, who he adored and who died when Martin was a teenager. It seems that it was after this that Martin started to go further and further off the rails, with no male role model in his life, a mother who barely knew what day it was and a grandmother who refused to talk to him openly about things. His grandma also had him on a pedestal, which meant that he grew up with a severely overinflated view of his own importance.

He told me that he was bullied at school for being 'different', which came from him always wearing a blazer, even though it wasn't necessary, and carrying a briefcase rather than a school bag. I think the outdated and old-fashioned upbringing he had, together with his own distorted sense of identity, had done him no favours and resulted in him becoming fairly socially isolated. It certainly all added up to make him the man he was, the man I now lived with, the man who I barely knew but who from the outset was trying to control my every move.

Once we were officially together things went at lightning speed. There were no discussions about the future, as Martin knew what he wanted, and I was expected to go along with it, showing gratitude and being flattered. The arguments were so huge I always wished I'd never said anything. Martin could manipulate things so well – I swear he could have stabbed someone a hundred times and still convinced everyone (including himself) that they had thrown themselves on his knife in order to make him look bad. That's how he worked. He lied so often and so efficiently that he stopped recognising what was truth and what was fiction and seemed to genuinely believe his own lies. In fact, he would be overly indignant whenever someone questioned the truth of a lie he'd told.

He was so volatile at the slightest thing that didn't suit him, throwing things, ranting and raving. It was like waiting for a firework to go off all the time. He would go from zero to full-on rage in seconds at the slightest little thing. Our relationship was more a cross between father and daughter, or owner and possession, than anything romantic or equal. I had no frame of reference for a healthy relationship after the messages I'd been given growing up, and this was all further reinforced by Martin saying that I should be grateful that any man would want me.

Very quickly my life became one of walking on eggshells. I guess I had imagined a picture of domestic bliss – nothing fancy or overambitious, just normal. It was a bonus to think that I wouldn't need to be embarrassed about where I lived or go hungry any more; I just wanted, at last, to have control over my own life. I wanted to pursue social work or write children's books, but he mocked all of that, so I quickly learned not to mention anything that would result in him making fun of me yet again.

Not long after we moved in together, Martin demanded that I stop work – this was odd, as he was my boss, so it couldn't have been through jealousy. I didn't realise at the time that it was just part of the way controlling men work, the way they cut you off from everyone and everything so that you think you can't cope without them. He told me that I didn't have to work and that I should be putting my efforts into supporting him. I was oblivious to a lot back then. I knew he called himself by different names and had ID for them too, but if I ever questioned anything that didn't sound right he would shout, belittle and mock me.

'What do you know about anything? Why should I answer to you? Who made you judge and jury?' he'd yell.

I played along with everything, not wanting to seem unsupportive or immature. While he was renovating the new club, he'd said he was having difficulties with some of the 'paperwork'. The tale he spun was long and complicated, but the upshot was that he needed me to apply for brewery accounts to supply the club in my name.

'Just talk to the reps,' he told me. 'Make out that your dad bought the nightclub for you and sign some paperwork.'

'How will that help?' I asked.

'Never you mind,' he said. 'Stop asking questions unless they're about how you can support me, for once.'

Before long, there were meetings taking place and I was being primed as to what to say. All I knew was that it made him happy and I felt like I'd done something good at last, so I did what was asked of me. Little did I know that he had signed me up to hundreds of thousands of pounds' worth of debt that he knew he'd never repay. He'd already done this with previous businesses and had what he thought was a tried-and-tested way of scamming the suppliers. He would order massive supplies of alcohol from breweries for whichever club he had – enough to supply the Hacienda ten times over, never mind his little backstreet dive. Knowing he had no intention of paying the bills for them, he would then sell it all at cost through the back door, to other businesses who were getting it for silly money, and pocket the cash. He did this in all kinds of false names and no thought was given to the fact that he was committing fraud or that he had implicated and involved me in his dodgy dealings without me having a clue what was really going on. Martin thrived on having large amounts of cash to wave around, quite literally. He would have thousands of pounds on him at any one time and a briefcase full of money on the go, but we were still short of the most basic things in the flat, like a washing machine or furniture. All his money went on flashy meals, hotel rooms, cars, pointless gadgets and sci-fi memorabilia. None of the belongings that I had lost when we moved in together had been replaced.

Martin always had to be the victim; nothing was ever his fault. If he ever did concede that he was at fault or in the wrong, it was only to garner pity or lay guilt trips on someone else. It was his idea, after having lived together for a couple of weeks, to try for a baby. It wasn't something that was on my agenda. I adored my nephews and niece but I didn't want to be that girl – I wanted to be different and travel and have a career. These goalposts were looking non-existent now though, as there had been that pattern of control from the day I had moved in with him – it was gradual but effective.

Anything that I wanted or hoped for that didn't fit in with his ideas was mocked, to such extremes that he would leave me in tears, feeling like a complete idiot for having any ambition or independent thought. He would make me feel completely worthless and foolish, always immature and stupid. That behaviour was so consistent that I soon relinquished all my own hopes and dreams and adopted his – taking on his opinions and going along with whatever he wanted to do in order to avoid being belittled and to get his approval. Martin was excellent at emotional manipulation, making me believe that I was overreacting to things, that I was a drama queen, or that he hadn't even said what I *knew* he had said in the first place.

It was, yet again, abuse. It had been there with Uncle Phil, it had been there with Mum and it was now there with Martin. It seemed as if almost every major relationship in my life had followed this pattern, but, while I was in the midst of it, I didn't know that.

You're so stupid.

How can you have forgotten that already?

Show a bit of gratitude.

Plenty of women would want what you've got.

Don't say another word until you've actually thought about this.

What are you accusing me of?

I never said that.

What are you talking about?

You're overreacting.

You're imagining it.

You're mental.

You've got a screw loose.

That didn't happen – what are you on about?

It was insidious, layer upon layer of questioning and doubt built up until I didn't know who I was. He manipulated me so effectively I thought I was going mad. He completely denied things that I had thought were true, saying that I was imagining things, or making me question whether I had got the wrong end of the stick yet again. I didn't know whether I was mad or stupid, but Martin certainly left me in no doubt that it was one or the other.

I had no self-esteem, no confidence, and he had me isolated from practically everyone. The only person I was allowed to trust was Martin – according to him. The only person who was looking out for me was Martin – according to him. The only person who knew what was right for me was Martin – according to him. The only person I needed in my life was Martin – according to him.

I ended up believing it. He was the source of everything in my life, so everything he said *had* to be true. My self-esteem and confidence had gone, not that there was much to start with, and I was becoming increasingly dependent on him. There is no doubt that the relationship was a toxic one, but I couldn't see it. The only life lessons I'd ever had were twisted ones, so I had no template of normality to judge this by, no idea of what should be going on between a man and a woman. Maybe this *was* what love was like – how would I know?

I tried to rationalise what he was doing and told myself it was just because he cared, just because he wanted the best for me. I would second-guess myself and apologise all the time. I would also wonder what I had done to make him react the way he did. Had I talked too much or maybe too little? Perhaps I'd been too loud, or my words had seemed critical. I wondered if I was dressed in the right way for someone with Martin's lifestyle – was I the right sort of partner for a man like him? Did I look the part? Was I pretty enough? Was I thin enough? Was I *enough*? I doubted everything about myself, questioned everything. As time went on, he would trivialise what I said, he would question whether things had happened, or whether they had happened the way I remembered them, he would say I was lying, that I was making things up, that I was an idiot.

I had minimal contact with my family by this point, as Martin would tell me repeatedly that they didn't care about me. I had told him some of what had happened to me, without detail and in a vague sense. This was used against me for a long time.

'It's because you're fucked up in the head,' he would say. 'Why are you bothered about scum on a council estate who don't care about you?'

I didn't miss Mum though; it was her I was running away from. I'd hoped that once I left home I would spend much more time with my brothers and sisters. This wasn't to be. Martin had decided which of them he liked, largely based on who voiced their concern that their little sister had quickly moved in with someone they barely knew, who was restricting contact. They knew what behaviours were out of character for me and must have been able to see the writing on the wall. I was nothing more than his 'yes' girl. He dictated what we did, where we went, what we ate, who I spoke to and how I dressed. He was clever – always stopping short of forbidding contact with people or laying down the law, he would just manipulate the situation and say that people were a 'bad influence' on me or 'filling my head full of crap', as if I were a small child. It would then be so awkward and uncomfortable to speak to that person, wear those clothes or do that activity, when he had put all of those doubts in my mind, that I would inevitably stop for the sake of a quiet life and so as not to upset him.

He was clever. He was very, very clever, as he had actually shown his true colours so early on and I had still fallen into his trap. I might get out – or it might get worse.

CHAPTER 11

Trapped

MARTIN HAD SAID that he wanted a baby only weeks after moving in together, but I'd seen all my sisters have families very young and, as much as I loved them, I wanted something different. I was a bit confused as well, as he showed so little interest in seeing his son – though he said he missed him; on the one occasion he was allowed to have him for a few hours he left the child with me and went off with his friend for the day. However, as the weeks went by he started to mention having a baby more and more, partly I think as he liked the idea of having a wife and family – but not the reality, it seemed – and partly as it was another shackle to him that meant I was less likely to just walk away. It went from being a conversation to being something that meant I didn't love him if I wasn't willing to do it, which was the usual pattern.

He threw my contraceptive pills in the bin and, on the day he had the grand opening of his club, only three months after we had got together, I found out I was pregnant.

It was as quick as that.

In retrospect, I can hardly believe it. Twelve little weeks, not even a hundred days, and I was trapped. My period was two weeks late and, although I just knew, there was still a sense of shock when I did the test. Martin was preparing to open a club in what is now a really busy part of Manchester but back then was quiet and mostly unused. He wanted me to sit in the booth at the front and take membership payments from people. On opening morning, I'd picked up a test from the chemist and quickly did it in the club toilet. As the two lines slowly appeared, I was shaking. All the talking, planning and imagining can't prepare you for the reality of discovering you are having a baby for the very first time; it's such a surreal feeling.

I was terrified, scared of even telling him, as I knew that once I did there was no going back. I was with a man I'd only known five minutes and suddenly it all seemed very real. I wasn't attracted to him, and really disliked a lot of his ways and actions, but I was also completely unsure whether it could still be love. I didn't know. I had nothing to measure it by. I felt protective of

Martin in a way, as I knew people were unkind behind his back (and sometimes to his face), and he made me laugh at times. He was unpredictable, which intrigued me, he was bizarre, eccentric, interesting and unique – all things I hadn't really come across before. I translated my fascination and his manipulation of me into thinking that I loved him.

He was extremely possessive, and if other men ever passed comment on me he would smile proudly at them but then go into a mood and tell me I had encouraged it, either by looking at them or by what I was wearing (which he always chose anyway). And he tried to turn the tables, always flirting with female bar staff to the point of embarrassment, asking if they were wearing bras and suchlike. It was humiliating but if I ever dared mention it, he would make out that I was insanely jealous. He seemed to almost get off on it. For years he made out that I was jealous, even although it actually became the case that I desperately hoped he would meet somebody and leave willingly.

Martin would go on and on about people flirting with him, which resulted in me believing that all his extreme behaviours were borne out of love for me and what I drove him to. When he smashed up the house and punched walls, I had driven him to it. If he openly flirted it wasn't him, it was my problem for being jealous. If anyone looked at me, though, that too was my fault and I didn't appreciate how much he loved me.

I guess I was in love with the idea of being in love and someone actually caring about me, so I buried my head in the sand and ignored the reality of the situation. I once found a list and description of escorts in his suit that he'd left me to get cleaned. Even faced with evidence (5' 3", Gemma, red hair, size 10, £30 an hour), he would tell me I was mad and that he'd put it there for a friend. At that point I didn't care what he did – it was the lack of respect that bothered me.

From the minute I found out I was pregnant, life changed. Any doubts I had held about our relationship were shelved. Now this HAD to work. I wasn't going to have a child as a single parent, go back to a council estate and live in poverty. That seemed my only other option, and so for someone who hadn't particularly wanted children I found myself desperately and intensely attached to the growing life inside my belly. I was determined to give this child the best of everything and give them every opportunity that I could. I would keep them safe and they would grow up in a house where they knew they were loved and weren't desperately missing one of their parents. They wouldn't be the odd one out with only one parent around, they wouldn't be dressed in dirty hand-me-downs and I would be a proper mum in every sense of the word.

I was a child having a child, but I was determined to be the best mum my baby could have. In my head it was so easy and idealistic. Martin was over the moon when

Trapped

I told him – there were bouquets delivered every hour, with teddies, balloons, chocolates. Seeing how happy he was made it easy to believe that everything would be good. In between deliveries, he was flirting with any girl who moved and making sure I was hidden away in my little booth, but I focused on the positives and all I could think about was what my baby would be like.

As soon as I told Martin I was pregnant he started to talk about getting married, claiming that he didn't want to have a child out of wedlock. It was an old-fashioned notion and just another way to have control over me. I was only just coming to terms with having a baby and getting married was definitely not something I'd given any thought to, definitely not something I viewed as a positive thing given my parents' relationship and the things I had witnessed.

Martin asked several times what I would say if he proposed and I always replied that the answer would be 'no', as I didn't want to get married while I was pregnant. Even with my age and inexperience, I could see that he gave no value to relationships in general, never mind a marriage. I'd also seen the way he had slept around before I got together with him, and I now knew that he'd been married the whole time. I was focused on my baby and, as his divorce had only just come through, thought he wouldn't push the issue.

I should have known he would get what he wanted – that was becoming the pattern. He arranged for us to go away for a few days to Morecambe with his mum and grandma. During the first night's meal, he grandly produced a ring in front of everyone.

'Will you marry me, Katie?' he asked. He said it as if it was the first time ever, and neither his mum nor his gran knew that we had already been through this. I grimaced as his mother wiped a tear from her eye. I didn't have it in me – as Martin well knew – to humiliate him, so of course I agreed, feeling sick to my stomach. I wondered what I had done wrong. I must have expressed myself badly when I'd told him – a dozen times – that I didn't want this. It must have been my fault. I was an idiot and a total coward. At the same time, I also felt bad for being a horrible person given that I was lucky enough to have met a man so kind as to want to spend his life with me. My head was all over the place and I just kept thinking that at least it would be nice for the baby and that it wouldn't happen for a long time anyway.

The pregnancy progressed well and there was no more talk of a wedding for a while. Martin's initial reaction to the baby had prompted me to think that I would be treated more positively, but the reality was different. He didn't like the look of my baby bump. He said he just didn't feel attracted to pregnant women. He said I was fat. He didn't like the feel of the baby moving in my tummy next to him at night. It irritated him, so I would end up perched on the edge of the bed so as not to annoy him. I was extremely tired all the time. We kept unsociable hours, up all night and asleep for much of the day, but Martin expected me to help in any way he demanded with the club as well as keeping the flat in order, while he played the big boss and flirted with anything with a pulse. If I ever showed signs of being exhausted he would shout that I was unsupportive and that he didn't know why he was with me. Very quickly, I started to feel completely worthless.

The baby was due towards the end of April and after Christmas he started to act even more cagey than usual. I never knew if he would come home or not. I spent much of my time in bed crying my eyes out, feeling completely worthless and unlovable. Nice things happen to nice people and bad things happen to bad people, don't they? That's what I thought. I'd been treated like a possession, a nuisance and an inconvenience throughout my childhood; now, my relationship with Martin was continuing that pattern. Everything reinforced to me that I just mustn't be a nice or good person at all and that I deserved bad things.

In February of that year, not long after I'd found those slips of paper with descriptions of massage services and escorts on them, Martin was particularly absent for a few weeks. I had little contact with anyone apart from him and his family, so I had very limited potential to build friendships. I was completely isolated, only seeing him, people he chose to associate with and his mum and grandma. I didn't have friends or drive or have my own income. He controlled everything, including me. I was completely dependent on him. Most of the time, we didn't even have food in the house; I would have to wait until he got home and brought some or took me to the shops. Towards the end of February, I was excited but also terrified at the prospect of the baby coming. It was hard to comprehend. I desperately wanted a girl. I wouldn't have been disappointed, I would have loved my baby regardless, but given a choice, I wanted a girl so badly. I wanted a girl to dress up, to protect, to give everything that I had felt missing from my own life.

As the month went on, I was having Braxton Hicks contractions and was completely exhausted round the clock. Left alone most of the time, I would just sleep. I wanted to prepare my baby's room and buy things but, other than a couple of generic outfits and teddies, we didn't have much at all as the money wasn't in my control. Everything was always left until the last minute with Martin. I never even knew for sure where we would be living. We'd moved out of the rented flat we had had and he'd rented a tiny one-bed annexe of a cottage, again in false names. In fact, I had to answer to the landlord in another name entirely that Martin had made up, for reasons I never understood – he would just say people were after him. It was here that I spent my days waiting for the baby to arrive, while Martin would come home as and when it suited him, sometimes staying away for days on end. As the absences went on, my mind was racing and I eventually had to ask where he was disappearing to, even though I was scared of what his response might be.

He looked at me as if he was trying to work out how to play this. I wondered what I was in for – would he put on the little-boy voice he often did when he wasn't getting his own way? Would he say that I would be better off without him, which was another angle he exploited for sympathy? Or would he even produce a bizarre gift, such as the pet monkey he had appeared with recently?

'I've been trying to arrange a surprise for you,' he began, as I prayed it wouldn't be another monkey. 'It's all gone wrong.' I breathed a sigh of relief at that. Not a monkey then.

The 'surprise' was that we were getting married in two days.

I hadn't wanted it. I had told him this fact many times – but he knew better. He had booked a register office in a different town and arranged everything. I was speechless. It was presented to me as the most romantic gesture in the world because he had wanted to marry me SO much and for our baby to be born to married parents. There was no room for my thoughts or opinions, it was all about him and what he wanted.

The next day I was taken to my mother's house so she could sign the papers she had to as I was still under eighteen – which she did without question – and we got married the next day with two of his friends in attendance. The following day we went to Alton Towers, with my massive baby bump and two of his friends. That was it. I was married. I went through it all in a daze. I know now that Martin was controlling me very skilfully, but then . . . then I was just shell-shocked.

Things were closing in on Martin. He was still trying to control me, but he couldn't control the fact that his fraudulent activities were catching up with him. Debt collectors and private investigators were looking to question him, as were the police. As March turned into April, I got a phone call from his business partner to say that Martin had been arrested.

It was 1990 and the local Strangeways riots were in full force. Images of prisoners stripped to the waist sitting atop the prison roof throwing tiles down were streamed out from our local news channel. It was a huge story at the time, with the riot lasting for a total of twenty-five days. After his arrest, and as my due date grew closer, Martin's business partner had me stay with him and his family while Martin was being held and questioned at the police station on several counts of fraud. It was awkward, as I barely knew them, but I had a few weeks until the baby was due and was hopeful that Martin would be home soon. He'd always said that no one could ever prove he had done anything wrong and that he was too clever to be caught.

It was a warm April and, a few days after Martin was

arrested, I watched the second day of the riots on TV and then went to bed. I was getting pains regularly and found them embarrassing in front of people I didn't know very well, so I wanted to sleep in the hope they would ease off. But things got progressively worse, and when Shirley – the lovely wife of Martin's business partner – went to bed, she came to check on me, giving me a hot-water bottle and telling me to wake her if I needed her.

'I'll be fine,' I reassured her.

I wasn't. Over the next hour, the pain became all-consuming, racking my whole body with every new wave. I was still sure that it was a false alarm but, when it got to the point where I could barely speak for the pain, I sheepishly went in to Shirley, terrified and crying my eyes out. She called a taxi and sat with me, stroking my hair and reassuring me. She came with me to the hospital, where I was told that I was 6 cm dilated and the baby would be coming soon. They took me to the delivery suite. I was in shock that this was really happening. Shirley sat holding my hand while I breathed through each contraction with gas and air. Several times different nurses asked if I had friends or family on the way, but Shirley just shook her head at them while they looked at me pityingly. The pain continued throughout the night and into the next day, when I was finally told I could push. Just as I was about to start the final stretch, Martin came running into the delivery room, dishevelled and smelling the worse for wear after several nights in a police cell. He was followed by his grandma. As he got to the bed, I gave my final push and my baby arrived.

There she was.

My girl.

My beautiful baby girl.

She weighed 7 lb 3 oz and had a head full of dark hair, pouting lips, dark eyes and a little bruise on her face. I couldn't take my eyes off her. I had never experienced such gut-wrenching, all-consuming, overwhelming love in my life. The strength of the love I have for my children can still take me by surprise, but then it was a totally new experience and I held her, sniffed her and wouldn't – couldn't – put her down.

Finally, the midwives persuaded me to have a bath. When I returned to the bed, they were singing 'Happy Birthday'! I hadn't even realised I had just turned eighteen – they were the only ones who had noticed, after looking at my records. Baby Katy was the best birthday present I'd ever had – I didn't need anyone or anything else. We would share a birthday and a bond for ever.

It was common in those days with your first baby to stay in hospital for five days. They also gave you the option of taking your baby to the nursery throughout the night so that you could recover and get some sleep. But I wasn't having her away from me for a second. I never put her down and just lay in bed for hours on end, staring at her in my arms, only putting her in her bed beside me when I could no longer keep my eyes open and my arm was weak with holding her. She must have had a million kisses before she even left the hospital. I was euphoric and didn't think that I would ever come down from my cloud. My relationship with Martin didn't matter, having no one didn't matter, not liking myself very much didn't matter, because now I had this beautiful baby girl who loved me and was dependent on me. She was the most perfect thing I had ever seen. I couldn't believe that she was mine and that nobody could take her away from me.

The morning after Katy was born, I woke in the hospital still feeling the same disbelief that she was all mine, and was filled with wonder that such a perfect little human had come from me. Something else was creeping in, though. I didn't know what it was and wasn't able to define or explain it for a long time, but it was sadness. Deep, heartbreaking, choking, crippling sadness. I continued to adore and love my new daughter, drinking in every detail of her and every new movement she made, but it was tinged with an overwhelming darkness.

Day after day, I lay in bed staring at her while crying and crying. The nurses were lovely and asked me what was wrong, sitting stroking my hair as they waited for my reply, but I didn't know. They said I had the 'baby blues' – maybe I did, as my mind and body were in shock just like most new mothers, but as time went on I found myself thinking more and more, for the first time since leaving home, about my upbringing and the things that had happened to me.

Looking back, I know I was experiencing a mother's love for the first time. As all the new emotions swarmed around my head, my will to keep my little girl safe and happy and always put her first made me realise how my own mother should have felt about me. The magnitude of her actions and lack of care for or emotional connection to me hit home like a sledgehammer. I didn't want to feel sorry for myself, and it wasn't self-pity — it was just another nail in the coffin of realisation that not only was I not lovable now, but I never had been. How could my mother have allowed anything like the things that had happened to take place? Why did she not want to protect me as I wanted to protect Katy? It played on my mind constantly. Up to that point, I had accepted my past and never really stopped to judge Mum or anyone else, but now I thought about everything more and more, remembering things I'd never thought about or had thought were long forgotten.

Martin and I were both besotted with our daughter, and though things were very difficult — we were staying with his grandmother and mum in a smoky, cluttered house, the police were investigating him, he was still playing mind games — we were probably the closest we had ever been and would ever be. None of his other actions mattered because my world revolved around my daughter now. While I was in hospital he had gone out to get all the essentials and I spent every waking moment with her, dressing her up like a little girl with a new doll, taking her out in her pram, brushing her thick dark hair and just watching her sleep. I was totally in love. As much as Martin clearly loved her, the extent of his input was to hold her and cuddle her. He didn't do feeds or nappies or crying, just the nice bits; that didn't bother me, though. I enjoyed every second of being a mum to Katy. It was only marred by the life we were now leading because of all Martin's dodgy dealings. He had closed the business, having run up hundreds of thousands of pounds worth of debt, and also distanced himself from his former business partner.

One day while walking with Katy in her pushchair to the nearby shops, I was stopped by a policeman who knew Martin. He told me to remove Katy from the buggy as he believed it was stolen. I almost laughed – I knew he didn't like Martin but this was crazy. He was serious though, and after making some checks on his radio he told me that the pushchair was being seized as he believed it to have been obtained fraudulently. Martin had got it while I was still in hospital but what he hadn't told me was that he had bought it on finance under a false name. He had no intention of ever paying for it. I couldn't believe it. I was shocked, embarrassed and humiliated as I stood in the road with passers-by watching curiously as I was made to remove my daughter and carry her home. Later that night, the police attended the house and removed more property that Martin had 'bought'. I felt like scum and that my time with Katy was being tarnished by all of his nonsense.

As Katy grew into a toddler we talked about having another child, so that they would be fairly close in age. It sounds crazy that I was prepared to have more children with him, but I had a firm idea of what I wanted for my children: a life with siblings where they were loved by at least one parent. And Martin was an only child and didn't want his own children to be lonely so, for once, we were in agreement. When Katy was six months old we decided to try for another baby and I got pregnant immediately. We were very happy about the new baby but, again, I was a little scared. I loved Katy so much that deep down I don't think I really believed that I could love anyone else as much. It seems laughable now, but it was a real concern for me at the time.

Martin and I both ideally wanted a boy this time but either way we were just happy to have a little playmate for Katy. The pregnancy was fraught with worry, as Martin continued to be questioned by the police. They were always turning up at his grandma's house and it got to the point that every time I heard a knock at the door or passed a police car on the street I felt physically sick. I was a nervous wreck, not helped by his tendency to over-exaggerate everything and his volatile temper. We would be sat calmly watching TV and if I said something – in complete innocence – that he didn't like he would hurl a glass or whatever was to hand at the wall, making us all jump out of our skins. Then, inevitably, it would be portrayed as my fault for winding him up. There wasn't a door or wall in his grandma's house without punch- and kick-holes in them. My home would be destined to have the same marks for the next twelve years.

We moved into the flat just before our next baby was born, as it wasn't possible or practical for us to keep staying at Martin's grandma's house. He'd decided that he liked the first flat we'd rented, so got a mortgage for another one in the same block. I wasn't consulted but was ecstatic to be moving out of a place where I was criticised constantly. I was trying hard to be a good, supportive wife but nothing I ever did was enough. I made him a meal in his grandma's tiny kitchen for our first wedding anniversary but he didn't turn up – God knows where he was. Everything I tried to do to bring us closer together was wasted and he managed to explain it all away, which wasn't difficult to do to someone who had no choice but to accept whatever was said anyway.

I prepared the bedroom for the new baby. Katy slept with us, as I could never be away from her for long and she would end up climbing out of her cot to come and find me anyway, so in the end she slept spooned up next to me every night. The day I went into labour, I still had unspoken concerns that Katy would be jealous and that I wouldn't love another baby as much as her. Martin was there this time, although he sat reading comics and falling asleep while the nurses were checking on me. After a trickier labour than I'd had with Katy, my gorgeous boy Joe arrived, weighing 7 lb 4 oz. He had the same dark eyes and pouting lips as his big sister, but fairer hair.

Joe was a placid baby who barely cried at all. I was so relieved to find that, as soon as I saw him, I felt overwhelming love. I hadn't thought it was possible, but I was just as enamoured with him as I had been with Katy. I held him for hours on end, staring at his little face that was always so expressive. Far from being jealous, Katy was ecstatic about her baby brother, who she quickly labelled 'Josie'. She decided he was her own personal property. If she heard him cry from another room she would come flying down the hall to try to ram his dummy in his mouth, pushing my hands off him. 'I do it Mummy, Josie wants me to do it!' she would say. Josie didn't have a choice! It was a happy time and I immersed myself in caring and playing with my two perfect little babies round the clock.

By now I was back in touch properly with Dad and his wife, June, who became a lovely grandma to the kids. Martin (strangely) didn't have an issue with me seeing my dad and I seized the opportunity to reclaim a relationship with him. He and June visited us throughout the years my children were little and we would visit them too.

It makes me happy to know that Dad escaped a life with Mum to find someone who loves him as much as he deserves. Although we don't see each other often, we usually get together for Father's Day and birthdays. He still keeps his beautiful gardens, beside the same house where I spent the first eight years of my life. And still smells the same.

The investigations into Martin were ongoing, and when Joe was a few months old, his case went to court, where he was charged with various counts of fraud and deception. We were told there was a possibility he would go to prison but nevertheless when he was sentenced to twelve weeks it was a real shock. I went home to the children feeling numb – what was my life? It never occurred to me to try to leave, I just thought this was it.

Joe was a dream baby, a gentle boy who was very laid-back. He had the sweetest nature and a smile that would melt your heart. Once he started toddling, he followed Katy around constantly, carrying out all her instructions like her second-in-command. Over the course of the following year, after Martin had served his sentence, things were fairly routine with him. I knew what was expected of me, but being a mother had given me a bit more confidence and the children were more important to me than anything Martin could do or say. He knew they were my priority and he was often resentful of it, making little comments.

While he had served a sentence for some of his crimes, there was still an outstanding case in relation to the fraud he had committed with the nightclubs, on a bigger scale. They had tried to make a case against me too, for the forms I'd signed for Martin, which went to court, but when the circumstances were heard the judge dismissed it all and told me in front of him to get as far away as possible from Martin. He said that he was leading a vulnerable young girl down an unfortunate path. He was right.

Christmas approached and I had seen little of my mother that year. I had last seen her at Uncle Graham's funeral several months earlier. He had died of cancer and I felt I owed it to him to go to the funeral. I still struggled a lot with my past. Although I didn't actively sit and think about it, I was extremely protective of the children, and was always hyper-alert to the way anyone was around them. Every milestone that Katy reached I would relate to my own childhood and ask myself the same questions in my head. Why? Why was I so worthless that my mother had allowed it all to happen? I knew that I couldn't move on until I had some answers, until I had faced her – but I didn't know where I would get the strength for that.

CHAPTER 12

Ghosts

INITIALLY, I PHONED Mum as I had such anxiety about seeing her in person to talk about the past. It was a few weeks before Christmas and I hoped that the sooner I spoke to her, the sooner I could relax. I hadn't intended to fully talk about the ghosts in my life yet, but as soon as I spoke to her she launched full force into bitching about everyone. When I didn't go along with it and agree with what she was saying, she started on me too, saying how she would never expect me to support her. That was the final straw for me – I didn't shout or scream but I asked her where my support was as a little girl who had been made to go with HER brother.

'Why didn't you try to stop it, Mum?' I asked, quietly.

She went crazy and there was a total frenzy of screaming down the phone, with plenty of swearing. I was a 'self-obsessed little bitch' who thought the world revolved around her.

'What makes you more special than anyone else who has had to deal with it?' she went on. It continued until the stream of obscenities turned into white noise. I looked at my children, who were watching me crying, and I put the phone down. That would be the last time I would speak to her for more than twenty years. I couldn't allow her to keep poisoning my life now that I had these little ones to care for. In a way, I felt calmer and had more clarity. I was never going to get the answers I wanted but I'd taken control and I wasn't allowing myself to be verbally abused by her any more.

Meanwhile the letters were coming from the mortgage company thick and fast. It emerged that Martin hadn't made a single payment since taking out the loan and they wanted to repossess the flat. He had even told them that he was under financial hardship as our daughter had cancer. He told me this as if it were perfectly acceptable.

'That's sick, Martin,' I said. 'Absolutely sick – how could you?'

He ripped down a kitchen cupboard and a glass got thrown against the wall. He then went on to rant about the fact that they were asking him for evidence of what he had told them, and that he thought it was outrageous they would even think someone would lie about something like that – this was the kind of thinking I was up against. It was ludicrous and twisted, but I couldn't say a thing or he would start smashing the house up and the children would be terrified. His screaming was perfectly normal to them by now – they didn't bat an eyelid and very often when things would be hurled at the wall they would say, 'Oh no, Daddy's thrown his drink again!' and start wiping at the wall with a tea towel. I hated that this was their normality, but also convinced myself that most people had hidden lives, marriages were a far cry from what was written in novels and, anyway, as Martin always said – who else would have me?

I was dutiful in every way I could be, but my focus was always the children and keeping them as happy as possible. Martin still didn't work but had a series of get-rich-quick schemes that ranged from sending out pirated copies of software to making the most basic of fitness books. All his scams made pennies and we survived on benefits. He could easily have got a job – he was an intelligent, if disturbed, man – but he point-blank refused to work for anyone else. If I suggested it, I was insulting him. I would have scrubbed toilets if it would give the children a better life, but I was still forbidden to work.

Later that year, I found out I was pregnant again. The children were still little (Katy was two and Joe was six months); it wasn't ideal as we had no money and still had the threat of the flat being repossessed hanging over us as well as ongoing investigations into Martin's fraudulent activity, but not having the baby wasn't even a consideration.

The pregnancy was more difficult than the previous two. I was huge for a start, as well as having two small children to look after and, having no help, I was constantly exhausted and felt sick and faint, but I had to carry on. We had to start looking for somewhere else to live as Martin had dragged the situation out with the mortgage company as far as they would allow. He had been exposed as a liar and told the worst lies to excuse not paying the mortgage and now the repossession was in motion. We would be homeless in a few months, with two small children and one on the way. On top of this, the legal case against him had escalated and he was due to appear in Crown Court to answer charges of fraud and deception for large amounts of money. His solicitor had said that he would more than likely go to prison again, this time for considerably longer.

I was induced when it was discovered I had pre-eclampsia and, after a quicker labour than the previous two, Alex was born. Weighing a hefty 8 lb 13 oz, he had the same gorgeous dark eyes as his siblings, little dimples in his cheeks and an angry scowl on his face like he had been disturbed in his comfy bed. The minute he arrived my blood pressure returned to normal and the panic was over. I was twenty years old and mummy to three children under the age of four. They were all totally adored by me, but there was no doubt that it was a lot to cope with.

The next six months were difficult. Alex had some health problems and I worried about him, worried that the other children would feel left out, worried that we soon had to move with nowhere to go, worried what would happen should Martin go to prison; I worried about everything. We eventually found a miserable house in a miserable street with rats running through the back garden, but at least we got help to pay the rent for it. Martin wouldn't have lived there otherwise but by now we knew for certain that he would be serving some jail time, so the purpose of finding a house was to have somewhere for me and the children to live while he was away. The children had bunk beds in one room while Alex had a cot in the bedroom with me, although he was such a cuddly baby that he inevitably ended up in bed with me anyway. We had only lived there a few weeks when, just before Christmas, his case was heard, and he got sentenced to two years in prison, on three counts of bankruptcy, gambling, and three counts of obtaining property by deception.

Initially I was devastated. He was the children's father and I did have some love for him. My life had revolved around him 24/7 since the day we got together five years earlier. I wasn't allowed to tell anyone where he was – the story if anyone asked was to be that he was 'working in America'. It wasn't really an issue as I didn't see or speak to anyone but, if I had, I would have been so ashamed that, at twenty-one, I had a husband in prison, three small children I was raising alone and was living on benefits. It was a new low for me.

But then something happened. Though I was under the stress of managing and living off a very small amount of money and trying to appease Martin, it was suddenly like a weight had been lifted. I didn't recognise it at the time, but it was an inner strength kicking in. I was determined that people weren't going to look at me or my children and be able to pass judgement or think I couldn't cope.

I got them into a routine, which had never before been possible because of the lifestyle we'd had. The priority was making sure they were dressed smartly and that I had food on the table. I organised my bills and found something of the girl I had been. Things were very hard, but I didn't have someone berating me every day, questioning my every move, and having to be answerable to someone who did whatever they liked with no thought as to how it affected me or the children.

Things became organised and, for the first time in a very long while, I was in control of my own life. Not always – most weeks I wouldn't be able to eat for several days, for as well as visiting him, Martin constantly wanted money sent to him to make life easier for him in prison. I was on benefits and my money was tightly managed but there was no option to refuse – he would scream and swear down the phone at me until I was in tears. I would send him whatever I could while making sure that the children had what they needed.

I guess I could have left while he was in prison, but I didn't. I still had no options, I was still determined that the best thing for the children was to have both parents and I didn't want to be the one to take that away from them just because I was unhappy with their dad. I travelled to see him every fortnight, taking several trains and then a taxi. He was in an open prison, so the rules were fairly relaxed. We were able to sit at a table for an hour or so before I would have to make the journey back; meanwhile he gave me instructions as to how he wanted me to look when he got home, even sending pictures of girls in magazines that he wanted me to copy. I wasn't overweight by a long chalk; in fact I was losing weight as I often went for days on end without food. Where others might have been concerned, he was thrilled at the weight loss. He never questioned whether I was okay or managing – his questions were all related to things that affected him. Had I been speaking to anyone? Had I managed to buy him the things he wanted? Had I been able to get some money for him?

When he was released, the house that had been good enough for me and the children to live in for the last year wasn't good enough for him. As soon as he got home I was instructed to start looking for somewhere else. That was fine with me as it wasn't a nice place, and with three small children, one who was due to start school, we needed more space and I wanted them to have somewhere they could have their friends round. We soon found a three-bed semi in a pleasant enough street that we rented with the help of housing benefit (though the story was to be that we had bought it, of course) and we moved in a few weeks after Katy started school.

It was a picture of fairly normal domesticity, but I'd tasted being in control of my own life and hated that as soon as Martin came home, he expected to pick up where he'd left off; he was belittling and criticising everything I did, said and wore and who I spoke to. I couldn't handle it any more – the difficulties I had faced alone were different. I didn't have the mental energy to go back to this and it soon started to take a toll on me. My life was no longer my own and I found myself feeling suffocated. On the back of everything that had happened to me was an overriding sense of worthlessness. It was just a deep dark pit of despair that was to last for many years, with the only intermittent light being the children's presence and my sense that I had to carry on being a mother to them.

I began to hate my reflection and would claw at my face when I caught a glimpse of myself. I would starve myself for days. There was no premeditation or plan involved; it was almost subconscious, almost a way of punishing myself for being unlovable but also a way of being a tiny bit in control of what was happening to me. Martin's constant comments about my appearance and his desire for me to be a size eight and weigh seven stone (long before it was fashionable) made me want to rebel and metaphorically stick my fingers up to him. He would analyse how much I ate and what I ate, commenting that I was having a lot, constantly asking me if I was on a diet and always criticising. If I said anything back, then glasses would be thrown, walls would be punched. The children were older now and much more aware of what was going on, so I did what I could to appease his temper and moods. I would give myself tiny portions of meals and hide a normal one away to have later when he would inevitably go out, doing whatever it was he got up to.

I don't remember what triggered it initially except for the constant dripping of criticism and the spiralling hatred I had for myself, but I do remember the night my eating disorder took hold.

Martin had gone out, the children were in bed and I ate the rest of the meal that I'd hidden away earlier. For some reason, this time I didn't stop there. I ate everything and anything that was in reach – even things I didn't particularly like. I worked my way through a fridge full of the children's packed-lunch contents for the week, crisps, biscuits, everything. I remember eating peanut butter out of the jar with my fingers and almost making myself gag. All the time I was eating I felt a sense of euphoric numbness; it's a really difficult feeling to describe. It was in a sense satiating the ongoing hunger, but I was also almost laughing inside because I knew how much Martin would despise me eating so much. Another part of me felt that I was winning because I wasn't that hungry little girl any more who had no food for days; I was in control. I clearly wasn't but I felt that I was.

That was the first time I had eaten to excess like that. When I finally stopped for breath and realised just how much I'd consumed, the panic and nausea set in. I felt utter disgust at the quantity I'd had, and confusion as to why I'd done it. There was panic that I needed to replace the things I'd had and at the terror of all the weight I was convinced would pile on overnight. Needless to say, I felt sick. My legs seemed to automatically take themselves to the bathroom. With no clear plan in my head, I threw up the contents of my stomach until my eyes were streaming and my knuckles were sore from pushing my fingers so far down my throat. While I knew it was disgusting, I was also so relieved that a crisis had been averted. There was a lingering sense of satisfaction that I'd eaten so much food and Martin was totally unaware. I had been in control and he would never know. It wasn't something I was proud of – or planned to repeat – but it gave me a sense of something for myself that most 'normal' people will struggle to understand.

While I had no more intention of doing it again than

I'd had of doing it in the first place, it was out of my hands. It was as if I'd taken my first hit of a drug and I found myself in a cycle of bingeing and vomiting on a daily basis. At first, I would starve myself all day and just do it in the evenings when Martin was out and the children were in bed. Every day I would tell myself that I wouldn't do it again and then, like a deranged junkie, I would consume huge amounts and be doubled over the toilet for hours making sure I was completely rid of everything.

I would drive round the shops picking up massive quantities of all the things I enjoyed, but never wanted Martin to witness me eating. I never really tasted the food anyway as it was consumed so quickly. I would hide it all until I was alone and then start the bingeing. In hindsight, my mental health was at an all-time low. I'd passed my driving test by this point, so I would be driving around and fantasising about accelerating off a bridge or into a brick wall. These thoughts would just pop into my head almost like a compulsion. I had no plan to take my own life – without the children things may have been different, but there was no one to look after them in my absence; I had considered that much and there was no way I was going to leave them. I just wanted to stop feeling so unhappy and I couldn't imagine anything ever changing. I saw no way out. The ghosts of my past were all around me, but I couldn't see the links, couldn't see the patterns of control and abuse in my life.

In the absence of anyone or anything else, bulimia became my dysfunctional best friend. Within months of that first occasion I was in a cycle of bingeing and purging up to twenty times a day. My hands were constantly sore, my throat was constantly sore, my gums were throbbing, I was constantly exhausted and suffering from gastric problems, but it was always there – something just for me that no one could take away. My secret. The knowledge of how messed up it was made me loathe myself even more, but you can't abstain from food. It's everywhere and we need at least some of it to survive. No matter how hard I tried or promised myself that I wouldn't do it again, I inevitably had to eat something. I seemed unable to eat 'normally'. The compulsion to eat until I physically couldn't swallow another crumb was so strong.

I had stretched my stomach so much that it also took larger amounts to feel genuinely full. It became my normality. The plus side for me was that I had started to lose a lot of weight. I wasn't big to start with, despite Martin's comments, but now months of purging everything I ate were catching up with me. I stepped on the scales once out of curiosity and was shocked, but very happy, to see that I had lost over two stone.

I am not going to state how heavy I was throughout any of this time – I think it can be immensely triggering for people to have different weights associated with being large or small. I think it is more important for anyone reading this to know how healthy (physically and mentally) I was rather than how much I weighed. Two stone lighter than my previously healthy weight meant that I was now very unwell.

I didn't have many people around me, but a few neighbours and playground mums commented on my weight loss as if it was a good thing.

'How have you done it?' they'd ask.

'Well actually, I spend every day driving round collecting enough food to feed a small village, then hide it until I can chuck it all down my gullet with the force of a speeding bullet. Then when my stomach protrudes like a pot-bellied pig and even swallowing my own saliva is difficult, I vomit up every last morsel until my eyes are streaming, snot is pouring from my nose and the acid in my throat from my empty stomach burns like fire.'

I wonder what they would have said. Of course, I took the compliments as they were meant. My own husband rarely saw me naked but, one evening, he walked in on me when I was in my underwear. At this point, I was considerably underweight and seriously ill, constantly dizzy, fainting and at my lowest ever BMI. He looked me up and down and said, 'If you shaved a bit off your bum and a bit of your stomach you'd look almost normal.'

That night I ordered an Indian set meal for four and consumed it along with the rest of the massive stash I'd already collected. Bulimia gives you certain skills. You learn to be very secretive, but that was something I'd had to be as a necessity all my life anyway. You learn to be resourceful, making sure you will have access to toilets, baby wipes, make-up and toothpaste whenever and wherever you eat. I learned which foods come up more easily, what drinks helped; it's a whole hidden underworld of despair and secrecy that robs you of health, dignity and the hope of ever leading a normal life. I'd been in its grip for many months when I realised and admitted I needed to get help. I was weak and cripplingly tired all the time. My life revolved around buying food, bingeing, purging and sleeping. It was starting to affect my ability to parent my children as I had so little energy. When they got home from school, I'd make their dinner and then lie down for the rest of the evening. They would sit next to me while I read them bedtime stories, but I wasn't able to give them the time and energy I had before – which exacerbated my self-loathing and guilt and made the bulimia worse.

I finally plucked up the courage to go to the doctor. I didn't know what I was going to say to him – I felt embarrassed and pathetic. He was, however, lovely and I managed to mumble that I'd been making myself sick, while trying not to cry.

After looking at my notes and seeing that I rarely went to the doctor for anything, he said he felt that the problem had been going on for a while and was probably a lot worse than I was describing. He reassured me it could be beaten and prescribed me some antidepressants that were also specifically used to target bulimia. I left feeling more positive.

I would like to say that I took the medication and the urges vanished and I recovered immediately, but that didn't happen. My mood seemed to lift a little on the tablets, but the only improvement to the bulimia seemed to be that it would now go in cycles. Whereas before it was ongoing, now it was as if I burned myself out and became so weak and tired from the constant binge/purge cycle that I wouldn't have the energy to do it for a few weeks. When I started to feel better I would fool myself into thinking that I was cured, but as soon as my energy levels went back up the cycle would start again. It felt hopeless.

This continued for over eight years. As my body became used to the treatment I was giving it, I became a high-functioning bulimic. I did everything I needed to do, took the children where they needed to go; I even started a part-time college course and would spend my lunch hour bingeing and purging before returning to classes. Periodically, it would lessen its grip and I would be sure I had beaten it, but it was very difficult to eat normally after patterns of behaviour that had lasted for years. I no longer had any sense of being hungry or full. If I ate anything at all the urge to get rid of it immediately was overwhelming. If I managed to beat the urge, I was proud of myself but also disgusted that I had allowed the food to stay in me. And of course, the weight crept back on slowly; my body was hanging on to every calorie I consumed in case I purged it, so I was now no longer losing weight. It is worth saying that throughout this period, as well as being underweight I was also (in medical terms) a little overweight. Looking at myself and being aware that I'd gained weight just added to me feeling like a failure – I couldn't even be a good bulimic.

It was a way of life for many years and I continued to try to beat it – I still took my medication, as I had been advised not to stop, and I would have periods of being in control; but the urges never went away and just when I hadn't binged for a considerable amount of time they would suddenly make a reappearance out of nowhere. My bulimia completely dominated most of my twenties and it was just another thing that added to my feeling of isolation and not fitting in with the rest of the world.

I was in a completely loveless marriage with someone who now often took his anger out on the boys. Rarely with Katy, but he was very rough with Joe and Alex, to the point that I had to scream at him many times to never touch them again. I was accused of mollycoddling them because I didn't pick them up by their clothes and throw them down. He was also cruel to them – I've lost count of the number of times the children cried because he never attended their school plays or events, and he was emotionally cruel too.

We argued so much and he would be so aggressive that they would go to their bedrooms or put their hands over their ears. I didn't understand why he wouldn't leave, especially as he usually had a girlfriend on the go, but he would always say it was in my head and that if I was going to split our family up then the children would know it was my choosing. Knowing that I was on antidepressants, he would also make comments about me being 'mental' or 'fucked up in the head', which was a reference to the fact that he knew vaguely that I had been unhappy as a child. Those were dark years for me, dominated by an unhappy marriage and an eating disorder, but illuminated by my three babies, who brought me love and laughter every day.

By my late twenties we were living pretty much separate lives; the only thing holding us together was Martin's constant emotional manipulation of the children. As part of my college course, I had to do work placements. One was at a special needs school for children with emotional, social and behavioural problems, and when they offered me a full-time position I jumped at the chance. It was an opportunity to have my own income. I was aware that, if I was ever going to be alone, I would need to be able to support myself and the children financially. I would never be able to rely on Martin for anything.

I was finally determined to do something to try to change my own life. I wasn't a scared, naive girl young girl any more. I was a mother and was bringing the children up pretty much single-handedly anyway. His emotional neglect of me and them had only made me stronger. As I began to regain a little control of my life I also began to slowly overcome my bingeing and purging. The weak emotional wreck of a person who hated herself was who he wanted me to be, I knew that now – it made me easy to isolate, control and manipulate. The person I wanted to be was organised, ambitious and someone my children could look up to. That's who I wanted to become. It wasn't easy or quick – I still had to deal with abuse, demands and berating from him on an almost daily basis – but, where it once set me back, it now made me more determined. Bit by bit I managed to resist the urge to purge after every meal; the gaps between episodes grew longer and when I felt the compulsion too strongly I learned distraction techniques and coping mechanisms. It wasn't a quick process but after more than eight years of the eating disorder being in control of me, I was finally in control of it.

PART THREE

CHAPTER 13

Love

I WAS STRONGER now and, despite Martin's continuous attempts to undermine my parenting, my appearance and my sanity, I was doing my best to keep up appearances for the sake of my children. In hindsight, they would have been far better off if I'd left him years earlier, but I didn't want them to experience the same heartache I'd felt when Mum took me away from Dad and my siblings, so instead I compensated for it by thinking it was best for them.

Martin and I were now living completely separate lives – he had opened other businesses, other clubs and bars, and he was always either there or asleep in bed at home, so I didn't have to deal with him. His job was the perfect excuse not to come home until six in the morning. So, as he seemed to think it was fine to be out all night, I decided to do it myself.

I had a babysitter sleep over (he later got her to spy on me and report back to him) and went out with a friend. I was determined not to get home before he did, so we went back to hers and drank wine and chatted. A little after 6 a.m., her phone went and we both smiled, knowing it was Martin. I got a taxi home and he woke the children up to say, 'Mummy has been out with her boyfriend.'

It beggared belief. Sometimes, on the rare occasion I was out with friends, I would call in to one of his bars. As he was never expecting me, I would almost always catch him with some young girl. He would orchestrate an argument in order to fit in with whatever lies he had doubtless told people – it was always transparent and pathetic. He thought he was far cleverer than anyone else, but I knew him all too well. I used to pray that he would meet someone and be willing to leave, but he clearly wanted it all and for no one to be able to blame him.

Martin was getting caught out more and more often. Even when his own mother passed away one New Year's Eve at a young age, he went to 'work' while I sat alone at the side of her bed in intensive care until the machines had to be turned off. I arranged the funeral while everyone sympathised with his loss, a loss so great that he couldn't even be bothered to pay the funeral directors and left them to come knocking on my door long after I made him leave.

Love

Once his mother died, he put his grandmother into a care home until she died too, two years later. I visited every two weeks and it was sad to see her decline and distress, she was so confused. He was rarely home, but when he was around, he made my skin crawl. As the children got older I was more and more convinced that they would cope with what I now knew was inevitable. They were old enough for me to explain things to them.

I finally got sick of his womanising and lies. I tried to reason with him and said that we would clearly both be happier apart. I was also careful not to lay any blame on him and to try to make it a mutual decision, but although he admitted things weren't good he wouldn't commit to us separating. It took a while, but I needed to keep pushing for it because his presence was now causing the kids more harm than good. It wasn't right that they should witness a loveless dysfunctional relationship with a man who never took an interest in their lives. Of course, it was tinged with sadness too, as I had spent twelve years with this man and had fought so hard to try to make it work. I needed to accept that I couldn't do it alone. The children and I deserved better. As far as I was concerned my life was about to start.

The children took it with resilience and probably with a certain amount of relief that they would no longer have to listen to their parents screaming at each other. Martin took the last of his stuff before putting on his little-boy voice and asking me if I was absolutely sure this was what I wanted. It was. As his car drove away and I closed the door after him I burst into tears. Tears that I hadn't made it work and given the children the perfect nuclear family, tears that I had wasted so many years on a lost cause – and tears of pure relief and anticipation. I was answerable to no one now. The children came back, and I sat them down and told them their dad had gone and now we all had to look after each other. After more tears it was like a huge weight had been lifted. We were almost giddy – it was like the last day of school. We played, we danced, we had food fights, and we laughed and laughed in a way that we hadn't been able to laugh for ever, because the atmosphere was always too tense, or Daddy had a crisis or Daddy was tired. It was like we had been released from our prison. It was a new start – we were free.

It was only in later years that I learned the name for what Martin had done to me – *gaslighting*. It knocked me for six. That was what had happened to me, that was something that had been done *to* me just like the abuse in my childhood had been done *to* me. I was just there, part of it, while Martin – like Uncle Phil before him – decided what control he would use. I was so used to being groomed that I had pretty much fallen into thirteen whole years with Martin. I had stayed with him despite his behaviour, the way he isolated me from people, the pattern he had of implicating me in so much of his illegal activity. I guess, initially, he gave me some self-worth by pursuing me relentlessly, and that was all I was used to – it fitted in with my worldview that had been forged when I was a little girl by my first abuser. When he was adoring and saying the right things, I could convince myself that it would all be fine, I'd end up in a fairy tale, but that was never going to happen. The only person who would ever save me would be myself. I had no bar; I had been taught that attention was all that mattered and that if someone paid some to you, be fucking grateful, Princess Kate. Maybe the lack of a sexual connection with Martin was comforting in some way, but I always wanted an emotional connection, and that was never going to happen with someone like him. I thought sex was something you had to do in a relationship, just to get through, and I never thought that would change. However, I did know that this was the start of a new chapter in my life, but I had no idea just what I was in for – although, finally, there would be so much light and happiness there, too. It came in the form of Paul.

I first met Paul on a night out with a friend. It was a quiet, girls-only thing with me and another mum from the school, not long after Martin had moved away. Paul was out with a friend and we got talking. Although it's a cliché, we clicked immediately. I was really attracted to him, which came as a bit of a shock as that hadn't played much of a part in my life. However, I had absolutely no plans to factor another man into my life – I'd only just got rid of the last one! I was enjoying my freedom, so, while we exchanged numbers, I wasn't looking for anything serious, and neither was Paul. He had been in a couple of long-term relationships but had never lived with anyone, and I had a husband barely out of the door. We texted and spoke on the phone and met up occasionally, but that was it. It did feel as if we had known each other for ages – he seemed lovely, although my radar wasn't exactly good in that department. As well as the physical attraction he seemed laid-back and calm, everything that Martin hadn't been. It was a rocky start, though, with neither of us being on the same page at the same time. He was convinced that I would end up back with Martin, and when one of us wanted to make a go of it, the other seemed to back away.

We were friends for months, on and off – I even told him about my past, in much more detail than I'd ever told anyone – but after a few petty rows we stopped speaking. Now I was single I was trying to enjoy myself by going out a bit, but I wasn't really interested in anyone else and found I was always comparing them to Paul. I couldn't stop thinking about him.

We reconnected a few months later and determined to continue as friends, but as soon as we met up I knew that I couldn't just be friends with him. We always seemed to end up kissing and hugging when we were alone. My feelings for him were growing and I thought it best that we stop talking for a while so that I could try to readjust my confusing – and quite scary – emotions. I texted him as much and he replied saying that he too had realised that he wanted more than friendship and asked if we could give it a go.

While my head was in turmoil – this wasn't part of the plan – my heart knew exactly what I would do. I weighed up the prospects of getting hurt again against the prospects of always wondering what might have been, and the heart won. From that day on, when we officially became a couple, we were inseparable. All the things that I had never believed were real were happening. I fancied him like mad, he was my best friend and he was a good, decent person. It took me a while before I could be comfortable introducing him to Katy, Joe and Alex, but once I did, he was great with them and I never had any flickers of doubt about him being around them, Katy especially. We did silly things like going to the park in the dark and opening the sunroof in the car to cover the children with snow while they all screamed laughing. We had fun and the children were finally seeing what a healthy relationship looked like.

Once we were serious, I felt it was only right to tell Martin. He acted all dejected and the little-boy voice came out again, but then he gleefully told me he had met someone too. I wasn't surprised at all by who the 'someone' was, as by my reckoning they had been involved for a while. It later transpired that he'd pursued her the same way he had pursued me when he was still married. I had nothing but pity for her knowing the lies he had probably told her and the life she had ahead.

Martin made life hell once he knew I was with Paul, constantly making threats and demands. Paul took it all in his stride. For the first time in my life I had someone prepared to stick up for me and stand by me no matter what, something I had never experienced before. At that point friends had always let me down, with no exceptions, but he never did. Two years after meeting we had our son, Oliver, and a year later, Paul proposed. It was wonderful to think that this amazing man wanted to build a life with me, and we began preparations for the wedding.

I had already told Paul what had happened with Phil, long before we had decided to marry. He was the first person I had really told all the details to, as I had never wanted to open up to someone before. After I did speak those words, tell those things, it played on my mind, but I kept shelving it.

I'd say to myself, 'Oh no, we're getting married, let's concentrate on that' every time I did think of it. I felt that when it came into my mind, I was dragging myself back to it and I didn't want that. I thought, just leave it, you're in a happy place, don't go back to that, Kate. I was the happiest I'd ever been now that I was with Paul, but

I did dwell on things from before and almost thought that I didn't deserve being happy. I would question myself a lot – why did I enjoy the misery, why did I keep dragging myself down? I felt I shouldn't be rewarded with happiness and that it would all go wrong anyway, so why sign up for even more horrible things?

I would have gone back to the past, back to what Phil did, at some point, but it turned out that it wouldn't be at a time of my choosing at all. On the night before my wedding, my sister Wendy was staying with me. We were having a few drinks and such a laugh, mucking about together like kids. We were lying in bed, giggling, chatting about everything, when she started the conversation that would change everything.

'I saw our Fiona the other week,' she said. Fiona was our cousin, and she was about the same age as Wendy, so they had always been close.

'How is she?' I asked.

'I have to tell you something but don't say anything,' replied Wendy. She'd been singing 'You're Getting Married in the Morning' to me moments before, but now, everything was about to be blown wide open. To cut a long story short, Wendy had been walking with Fiona one day as our cousin was going back to stay at her house. The barge Phil lived on was nearby, boarded up, and when Fiona saw him outside it she had frozen.

'What's the matter?' Wendy asked, and Fiona went to

213

pieces. When they got home, she told Wendy that Phil had abused her as a child. She was in a complete state, as she hadn't seen him for a while – she didn't live near him at that point. She was shaking and crying, which was completely out of character, as Fiona was usually very together and not an overly emotional person at all. Fiona eventually said that Phil had raped her when she was three and it had affected her ever since, unsurprisingly. She was such a lovely, caring person, and the damage Phil must have done to her was overwhelming. I felt devastated for Fiona as Wendy told me about the abuse Phil had inflicted on her.

'I thought it was just me and Michelle,' I said to her. 'I didn't know he did it to others.'

'What are you talking about?' asked Wendy.

It was as if time stood still. In that moment, as I lay there with my big sister on the night before my wedding, it all came back to me. I had assumed she knew. When my other sister, Debbie, had made a crude comment years before about him using us as 'glove puppets', I had thought everyone in our family, all my sisters, knew what he was and what he had done to me. My shock at this point was that he had done it to Fiona as well, that he had gone beyond the part of our family where Michelle and I were.

I thought Wendy was as aware of it as Michelle and Debbie had been, but that wasn't the case at all. I told Wendy all about how I had spoken to Michelle years later about it all, once I had left home and was married.

'Michelle told me that when she was at the riding school one day, Phil tried to perform oral sex on her. She kicked him, ran home and told Mum, who basically gave her a mouthful and played it down, telling her that she didn't have to go any more. She sent Michelle to her bedroom,' I told Wendy, 'and came to me that night, telling me that, as I wanted to go horse riding all the time, now was my chance. It was years later that it all made sense, Wendy, but he wasn't in our lives by that point.'

She was shocked, I could see that – but she still had questions.

I went on to tell Wendy that years later, on the phone, Debbie made the comment about him using us all as glove puppets, but it was almost as a joke. 'She said it in such a crude and unfeeling way, Wendy, that I was shocked. Even though we were never on the same wavelength and I had always wondered whether everyone had known what had happened, this kind of confirmed it. She didn't say just her, or just us, she said, "us all" and, for me, that was confirmation everyone knew, and it had been accepted back then. She made it sound like he had abused all the girls in our family, so I thought you knew.'

Wendy became hysterical.

'What are you saying to me, what are you saying to me?' she kept sobbing. I was crying, and Wendy was holding me like a baby. Finally, we both ran out of tears.

215

'Go to sleep, you're marrying the man of your dreams tomorrow,' she said to me.

I didn't sleep for ages – but I finally realised she was right: *I'm getting married tomorrow, best not have bags under my eyes!*

It was a lovely wedding – my brother Andy gave me away – but 'it' was there; from that night before my wedding, all I could think of was doing something about 'it'. I couldn't get out of my mind the thought that Phil could still be doing this, doing it to other little girls. I won't lie though – I didn't suddenly just set up a plan and stick to it. I didn't suddenly lose all of my fear and shed the years of conditioning. It took me a while. I picked up the phone to the police so many times, never daring to actually say the words, never daring to even think what those words might be. Finally, though, I did it. The truth was, I didn't really think anything would come of it, but at least I would know I had reported it, even if I was really just logging it in case any other reports were made. I knew now that there were generations of assumptions, secrets and lies – even I had made assumptions – and I thought, *I can only do what I can do. If I know I have told someone, that's right for me.*

I knew he wouldn't have stopped but I felt so stupid calling the police. I thought they would just ask what in the world I expected them to do after all this time. I needn't have worried. They were lovely from the second I reported it – they never made me feel disbelieved, they never made me feel it was unimportant; they were so good.

Naturally, everything came out in the family – I told everyone what I was doing, and asked Wendy to tell Fiona.

'I won't name other people, but she needs to know,' I told her. It wasn't long before Wendy got back to me and said Fiona thought I was really brave and she'd contact the police too. Michelle said she'd be with me every step of the way, and she kept to her word. Debbie said she was proud too and that she'd tell the police everything she knew, but actually, she called Mum immediately and said, 'The shit's hit the fan.' I have wondered about that a lot, wondered about how she chose to deal with it, but I guess that was how she finally managed to get our mum's attention and, to some extent, affection. She chose her side, when I hadn't wanted there to be sides at all.

It was eighteen months until the trial began, and those months dragged by. The police told me when they were going to speak to my mother, that they could only speak to her at home, they couldn't arrest her, and they were limited in what they could do. They said that, had the case been current, she would be done for child neglect, but there were different laws to consider due to the timescale.

They raided Phil's barge and found no material, no evidence as such, but he still sang like a canary. He was actually very amenable to them, saying, 'I've been waiting for this for a long time.' I'm not sure how he could square that with his view that he was only giving children what they wanted. Had he denied it, we would have struggled, but the police felt that they had a strong case because of the detail and there were many consistencies in our stories from when we were interviewed separately. Phil gave them more information and lots of instances that we didn't even know about, and was deemed to be an 'opportunistic' paedophile.

He was charged with twenty-six counts from his own mouth.

Those eighteen months of waiting were horrible even though the police were very good. My mother admitted nothing, and I had to deal with the fact that I just wanted to see some maternal feeling in her. I still wanted her to be a mum.

When the police turned up, she just said, 'Oh God.'

'Your daughters have made these accusations about your brother,' they told her.

'It must have happened then,' she replied.

I was better without her in my life – as had always been the case, really.

CHAPTER 14

Guilty

ON 2 NOVEMBER 2005, I sat in the small courtroom at Manchester Crown Court. Opposite there was a handful of journalists taking notes and periodically throwing sympathetic looks and reassuring smiles my way. Someone reached over to pass me a tissue. I didn't realise why until I felt the tears drip from my chin. I hadn't realised I was crying. All I felt was numb. I had seen him before I walked in, felt a burning on me. I knew someone was watching me and my skin started to crawl. I looked up and there he was. Phil. He looked the same. The same hair. The same face. The same eyes, boring into me. Now, it was all going to come to a head.

As the prosecuting barrister related our life story and a lifetime of our secrets to the judge, all I felt was relief.

Now it was out it could no longer fester in my head and poison everything I did. It had no control over me any longer. I was about to be free.

I had zoned out for a moment and only came back into the room when there was a collective gasp from everyone in the room at what the barrister had just said. Even the experienced and respected judge looked taken aback; the journalists were shaking their heads in disbelief.

My Uncle Phil had confessed that when he was not able to gain access to children, he would use his Great Dane dog for sexual gratification instead. He sat expressionless while the statement was read.

The statement that had been read had come from the defendant's own mouth. Why he would unnecessarily offer that sort of information was anyone's guess. But he had – and everyone could see what he was: a foul, disgusting man, only concerned with his own perverted desires.

As soon as I had started this process, I had known it would be highly unlikely that Mother would be held accountable for anything and I had tried to get my head into place with that. I had also known that Phil would get a custodial sentence as he had admitted everything, but there was a shock when one of those assumptions proved to be false, and Mother was indeed mentioned in court. That meant so much to me. I just wanted to hear it, for it to be recognised. I just needed it to be acknowledged. Once they did, it was enough.

Guilty

Once all of the words had been spoken, it was time to wait. I looked at Paul, at the man I loved, who had shown me such love, and I knew I could do this, I could cope with whatever was going to be decided. Phil was to my right, behind me. I had to turn to see him, and I managed to do that. I actually made a point of looking at him periodically. He was expressionless.

When it came to summing up, I really felt that the judge put into words how each of us had been affected and understood the impact the abuse had. He told Phil that he had been someone we should have been able to trust and feel safe with. He also said that while he believed he was an opportunist – and that the opportunity had clearly been provided by Mum – he could have removed himself from the situations. He *chose* to keep putting himself in situations that he knew would hold 'temptation' for him. The Judge acknowledged Phil's immediate plea of 'Guilty' and the fact that this had spared us the distress of a trial, but also said that due to the length of time the offending covered, he would have to impose a long sentence.

Ten years.

He gave him ten years and a place on the sex offenders register for life.

Uncle Phil showed no emotion. As they were ordered to take him down he turned to pick up the book he had with him and I felt almost a stab of pity. I know that sounds perverse. I actually felt sorry for him. I thought,

I know where you're going with that; I know where you'll be reading that. He looked so tragic and that book would be his only company that night, his only company for many nights. I don't know why I felt that way as he deserved everything he got. I think I felt that he might die in prison and that was what affected me. All of the judge's comments were spot on; he really got it. He said something about each one of Phil's victims and each one of his comments was really accurate. He said that he thought I had been a 'lost soul'. I had. I really had. I guess the judge knew everything that had been recorded by the police.

Phil's arrest was a catalyst for him to unburden himself of the guilt he had been been carrying, as I found out so much of what he had admitted to at the summing up. He knew it was wrong but said it was an illness – that was how he portrayed himself, as someone who had an affliction that he didn't want. He needed to be seen as a victim too. He told the police that he had only ever 'soothed' us and that he had only done things we wanted. We were children and he tried to make us complicit in our own abuse. I guess that is an illness of sorts. It's certainly twisted. All he had done was dress up 'asking for it' in a prettier package.

He looked like what he was as he was taken away – a sad creepy old man who had nothing and whose innermost secrets had been exposed. There was no joy, no feeling that I had 'won'. The press who were there and had listened to all the painful details of what he had done to us – and to his dog – were nodding in satisfaction. I don't think any of us expected him to get so long and we were grateful that the gravity of what he had done had been recognised, as well as Mum's role in it.

We all dispersed afterwards, and I called the rest of my brothers and sisters to tell them of the sentence. As the person who had opened this can of worms I wanted to be the one to tell them. Everyone else went home but Paul and I went and sat in a bar until later that evening to process events and have a bit of time before returning home to the children.

The free paper I saw on the tram on the way home had a small matchbox-sized piece about the case and the sentence. I thought about Phil spending his first night behind bars with years stretching ahead of him. I still felt some pity, but this was the first night that I also felt complete peace.

There were, however, other parts of my life that still dragged me back to my past. My sister Debbie and I had a relationship that was hard to define. On the one hand we were close. I loved her, and I knew that she loved me. On the other hand, I often felt a sense of resentment from her, that she felt I was favoured as the youngest and had had opportunities and things she hadn't.

I think she felt some guilt about the fact that she clearly knew Uncle Phil had abused me and Michelle, and maybe as we were younger than her felt she could have prevented it – I don't know. She had undoubtedly had a lot of trauma growing up. Mum left with us when Debbie was only sixteen, pregnant and very unhappy; it must have been so hard for her. Years later she went on to have a stillbirth after going two weeks past her due date. It was a baby girl and she was totally devastated. She had the horrendous trauma of a funeral after nine months of pregnancy and all the planning, and I think that marked her for ever, as it would any woman.

As adults we weren't as close as we had once been but kept in touch with phone calls and birthday cards. Things had become a little strained following the court case and my decision to come forward after she firmly laid her flag in Mum's camp. I bore her no ill feeling for that; she had spent her whole life wanting our mother's attention and approval; she needed it desperately, and I understood.

When Phil was convicted I made sure Debbie knew it was for all the things that she had suffered too but, now in her early forties, she had something else to contend with. She was diagnosed with cervical cancer. After what was thought to be successful treatment, it returned and Debbie was told it was terminal.

As a family we were in shock. Debbie requested that everything stay as normal as possible and I tried to adhere to that. I took the children to see her while she was still at home and doing reasonably well. She had lost her hair and was clearly very poorly, but at one point we spent a nice day together and I felt like we had our old bond back. Eventually she was moved into a hospice and it was apparent that she was close to the end. She was struggling to eat and drink and was shutting down. I had been to see her at various stages in other hospitals but since she'd been in the hospice I had been made aware that Mum had taken up residence and was sat at her bedside around the clock. I hadn't seen her in twenty years and had no desire to change that – she had put the final nail in the coffin when the police interviewed her and there would be no meaningful building of bridges between us now. But I needed to see my sister. The only way to do that would be if I accepted that I would have to lay eyes on the woman who had caused so much pain in my life. It took a while, and I beat myself up for not seeing Debbie sooner, but I finally went.

I felt sick. The minute I saw her face every ounce of me wanted to ask her *why?* Why was she reinventing history, sat there playing the doting mother with Debbie? Why had we not been worth caring about and protecting when we were little? Why? Why? Why?

I did spend some time with Debbie and the final time I saw her I told her I loved her and to sleep well – she passed away the next day with my mother at her side. It had taken her death for her to get any semblance of attention from that woman. It was clear that Mum hadn't changed, as she continued to play my sisters off against each other, causing friction and bad feeling. She admitted to one of them that she could only cope with one of her children at a time – I couldn't help but think that maybe she should have stopped at one if that was the case.

Needless to say, we were all distraught at the funeral – Debbie was only forty-five and should have been looking forward to her sons getting married and to becoming a grandmother. It just wasn't fair, especially when Phil and people like him were living into their old age. The day passed in a haze, as I think is probably normal when you lose someone so close to you. I was inconsolable, and my heart broke for my nephews.

At the wake I passed my mother on the way to the toilet. Unbelievably, she stood in my path and reached out to give me a hug. It wasn't the time and place to do anything but be polite and respectful, so, stiffly, I accepted. She made vague comments about the possibility of something good coming out of it, but it was too little too late. I had seen for myself the way she continued to treat my sisters and I wanted no part in it. My life had been better without her.

Since I had been with Paul, I had worked in a range of special units and schools. I knew that I was drawn to this type of career because of what I'd experienced but, to be honest, I had never really delved into that side of things. Yes, I was a survivor, but that meant that I was sometimes *just* surviving from day to day. I couldn't spend every minute of every hour looking into my reasons for everything, I couldn't always be looking for justifications – sometimes, I just had to be. I just had to go with what felt right, and this did. It was difficult work, but I hoped to be able to make a difference to these kids.

Some places were for children with autism, some were for kids with emotional and behavioural problems due to their own traumas, and some were for physically disabled children. It was demanding but so rewarding.

I struggled with wanting to make everything right for them – that is, of course, an impossible task, but many of them were going home to such awful situations that I found it hard to leave work behind at the gates. I worried a lot even when I wasn't there. It's been ongoing since I was little that I hate to see anyone genuinely upset. I automatically want to comfort them and make things better, and feel hopeless when I can't.

However, physically, I was feeling horrendous. Work was hard, not just because of the struggles of dealing with such difficult situations, but because I was permanently exhausted. I never felt right, I never felt well. Finally, I was diagnosed with ME. I was happily married, had seen Phil imprisoned, so no longer felt sick every time I passed someone with white hair, and I was pretty content, but my illness had been creeping up on me for years, a gradual process of becoming more and more tired; things that once were easy were becoming difficult. I was struggling to manage work and I could have slept 24/7. Everything hurt, every part of me, and

I spent a lot of the time thinking I was coming down with something without anything ever appearing. My joints hurt, I was forgetful, I had constant headaches. A multitude of tests and X-rays found nothing. After several years, by a process of elimination, I was diagnosed with ME/fibromyalgia/chronic fatigue syndrome. There are some medical professionals who say these things are all different complaints and some who say they are as one. Whatever it was, it completely debilitated me, and I was no longer able to work.

The doctor said it was probably previous trauma, which I found hard to understand as I had come through so much and things were now good. But I learned that this is common – people who have endured a lot of stress and trauma often only grind to a halt when their problems have passed. It's as if our bodies are in fight or flight, and when we know we have to keep fighting, we keep on going. Only now I could relax, and my body had decided that it'd had enough, the batteries were empty and all the internal pain I had felt for so many years had emerged as very real physical pain.

It was such a strange feeling. The kettle was too heavy for me to lift. I couldn't walk downstairs without resting every couple of steps. I felt like an old lady. Added to that was having to cope with people's judgements and prejudices.

'Oh, it's that "yuppie flu" isn't it?' they would say, rolling their eyes. I definitely wasn't a yuppie and it was nothing like flu. It was horrific and, at a time when I should have been happy, I was beside myself that this was the extent of the rest of my life. Bedridden and sleeping. I felt like I was waiting to die.

There is no cure for ME. They give you antidepressants, anti-inflammatory meds to help with joint pain, and offer pain management, the extent of which is really to not do too much but not do too little. It was a very dark few years when I felt that life was passing me by, but I had overcome worse and I worked hard to manage my symptoms. It is very tempting when you have been in bed for five days and then wake with a little glimmer of energy to try to make up for lost time, clean the house, visit friends, achieve things, but that inevitably puts you back to square one and it becomes a vicious circle. Though I did fall into that trap at first, I quickly learned and I stopped beating myself up for being tired and sleeping. I also noticed that mental exertion took a far bigger toll than anything physical. Over the next few years, with ups and downs, I became stronger and bit by bit reclaimed some life. I started working part time in retail so that I could leave the job at the door and, though it wasn't as fulfilling as my previous work, it was what I needed. I loved meeting people too, and at least I was socialising.

Eventually I felt like my old self and the need to feel like I was doing some good was always present. I started looking for something full time and saw a vacancy advertised in a psychiatric hospital. It looked really interesting and, after reading the person specification, I applied and subsequently got offered the position on the basis of my experience in working with challenging young people.

The people I met there changed my life. It was an intense environment and a world that most people rarely access. From the moment I started, the patients resonated with me. I saw myself in so many people and knew that it could so easily have been me, or any one of us. I understood their cries for help, their self-loathing and utter despair at the world that had dealt them such terrible hands. Many people still imagine straitjackets and electric shock treatment – that is a thing of the past, but what goes on behind those locked doors is still surreal and heartbreaking. I had entered a whole new world that I never knew existed and, in doing so, found many amazing dedicated staff – and many failings and many despicable staff who took pleasure in gaining control over the most vulnerable people imaginable. I stumbled upon a system that is so outdated, so broken and so damaging that I eventually felt no longer able to be a part of it. I had spoken up for myself and now it was time to speak up for others. Their truth needed to be told.

CHAPTER 15

Lee and Beth

DO YOU LIKE SEX?'

It was my first day and I was being shown around the Psychiatric Intensive Care Unit, or PICU, where I was working as a senior mental health support mentor. It was a secure unit, designed for young people between the ages of twelve and eighteen who had been sectioned for their own protection under the Mental Health Act. These were very poorly young people who were at immediate risk of hurting themselves or someone else.

'Do you?' the boy asked again.

'Ignore him,' said the colleague who was giving me a quick tour. 'Just ignore him.'

I looked at the boy who had asked me the question and made a quick decision about my response. He was about 5' 3" and skinny as a rake, with a huge head of curly clown-like hair and trousers halfway down his bum. He had his boxers on show like it gave him some kudos, and he seemed completely and utterly lost behind it all. He stared intently at me, mischief in his eyes, standing in front of me, barring the way down the corridor.

'I'm a gangster, bruv – cheeeese. Do you like sex or not then?'

He was ridiculous – but he was a kid.

'Depends who it's with . . . but not as much as chocolate,' I replied.

He looked at me, shocked, then his pale face broke into a huge grin and he started laughing. He moved out of the way while I finished on the ward. I could hear him periodically telling people who went past, 'She likes sex, but not as much as chocolate!'

Lee was sixteen that first day I met him, but he looked about twelve. Small in stature, he displayed overtly sexualised behaviour and language but, if you faced him off, he would become embarrassed and retreat. He wanted to feel that he was embarrassing you and that it was a taboo subject. He persistently dry-humped inanimate objects. The floor, a chair, a cushion. He was a tiny person with a huge character and it took a lot of the ward resources to manage his behaviour. He presented as an immature, oversexed little boy but his file told the real story.

He was from the south and still had a bit of an accent,

and he was a heroin baby. He had been born to an addicted mum who continued to inject herself while she was pregnant. As a result, he had to be weaned off drugs when he was born and had suffered developmental delays. Lee had been placed in foster care when his mother had been hospitalised for an overdose and he was found hungry, dirty and alone amongst filth and needles. He struggled to concentrate on things unless it was something that he was really interested in, such as football – at other times, he would appear to be in an almost trance-like state and would stare into space for long periods of time.

He was on all kinds of medication – mood stabilisers, antipsychotics, things to lift his mood, things to lower his mood. This poor kid had been in foster care with a nice family where he had been happy for a while, but as his behaviour became more sexualised it became risky as they had daughters in the house, and they had to let him go. As he had no real sense of how inappropriate his behaviour was, the rejection was hard for him to handle. The family obviously loved him and they kept in touch, but it was a long way to travel, so visits were rare. It was the same situation with his mum. In the two years that he was there, I saw her come twice.

I learned that this is a huge problem for mental health patients, especially younger people. There are so few facilities and beds that patients are often placed hundreds of miles away from their area, friends and family. This only exacerbates their condition and anxiety, and Lee certainly had a lot of anxiety. His foster family had been a black couple and although he was a white boy he aligned himself with and related much more to black people. He loved the young black male staff, who would talk about rappers with him and play football; it was when he was happiest. He even spoke in street slang.

We worked out that his sexualised behaviour seemed to stem from witnessing his mum being prostituted. Lee was only a toddler when he saw it, and the reports suggested that his mum used to sedate him with medication in order to keep him quiet while she had 'punters' back at their home. God knows what that child had witnessed. His anxiety was at its peak when he was waiting for a phone call from her – he would wait and wait and if she didn't call when she said she would, which was often, his anxiety would grow. He couldn't and wouldn't verbalise that he was worried, he would just start acting up. Ultimately, he was scared that she wasn't calling or answering because she was lying dead somewhere from an overdose.

Lee's stature meant that he was easy to restrain. Putting your hands on a patient to restrain them is meant to be a last resort when they are being violent towards themselves or others and all other techniques have failed. The truth is that for many staff members, this largely depends on the patient. The ones who are big and strong and take three or four people to restrain them are the

ones the staff are less likely to put their hands on –
whereas Lee, although stronger than he looked, was easy
to overpower. Every time he played up a bit or got loud
or bored, he was threatened with seclusion. He sensed
the injustice of this and would become verbally abusive
and – understandably when people were so quick to
grab him and try to restrain him – he would lash out in
any way he could; kicking, and punching anything in his
path. All he wanted was to go home – back to the area
he was from.

Lee, like so many others, was a lost boy. It is so easy to
label these kids. It's really convenient to say they are just
a certain way or that their behaviour ticks a certain box,
but Lee wasn't a box to be ticked, he wasn't someone for
whom there were easy solutions. He needed time and
love and boundaries and understanding. You don't get
much of that with temporary contracts and minimum
wage.

Placements were found for him several times in various
locations across the country but, as soon as his moving
time got close, his anxiety about moving would make
him act out and the placement would be cancelled, as
he would be deemed 'unsettled'. This happened time and
time again. Lee would get his hopes up only to be let
down at the last minute every time. He spent months and
months on the high-dependency corridor with no access
to the outside or interaction with other patients. This
was more to stop him antagonising other people than for

his own wellbeing, as he would constantly call out silly comments to people, and staff resources would be used in breaking up fights or separating him from others.

The way he was restrained was getting more and more violent. Anticipating what was going to happen, he would start throwing punches and would end up with six or seven people on him holding his head, arms and legs, so that it was impossible for him to move. He was expected to calm down while being held like this. Underneath the bravado he was such a caring lad who found emotions difficult. If he was scared, or sad, he played up and became hyper to distract his own thoughts. If he thought someone else was sad, he would find it intriguing, constantly asking if you were going to cry. I saw him weep many times towards the end of my time with him, but only ever when there had been countless people dragging him to seclusion and pinning him to the bed in restraint. Afterwards he would lie on the hard block that was meant to be slept on and, through the viewing window, I'd see the tears roll silently down his face. It was heartbreaking. He found it very hard to feel certain emotions, let alone show them, so when he cried I knew his distress must have been acute.

There is no doubt that he was a very complex character with challenging behaviour and many needs but, reading his file, it was plain to see why. He was treated like a prisoner by many people. This is a boy who often thought that staff were trying to poison him when they made him a drink. He knew that when his mum gave him things as a child he would become sleepy and he had subconsciously carried those memories with him. His medication could make him drowsy, but he was convinced that it was staff poisoning the milky coffees that he loved. Lee wasn't a danger to himself as such – he had never tried to deliberately hurt himself – he just had little sense of danger and was extremely vulnerable, easily led and open to being exploited. That was unlikely to ever change.

A psychiatric unit is meant to be a temporary measure, but Lee's difficulties couldn't be treated with a short course of intervention and medication. There was simply nowhere else for him to go. There was no place for a damaged boy who was alone and lost in a world that he just wanted to belong in.

Lee wasn't the only broken child I dealt with, far from it, but he has stayed with me. I could have been him, I could have been any of them, because the horror of what I went through with Phil and my mother (he was no longer an uncle to me, she was no longer a mum – I wanted, and needed, distance from them), could have tipped me over. The bulimia had been awful, but I had that under control. Looking at Lee, and the others, made me realise just how superficially we judge children. We label them so quickly, we decide what they 'are' in such a rush, then we treat them according to those labels.

I want to be at the front of the battle for people who

have slipped through society's safety net and found themselves in a world they never even knew existed, a place where no legislator passes helpful laws, where no police officer hunts down the bad guys. A place a lot of people would prefer to keep hidden, because if we uncover what really lies beneath the surface, what does that say about the true value we place on the most vulnerable in our society? Children who are abused, women who are controlled, vulnerable people who are given so little help that they see no future.

I needed to do something and, for every day I worked with these children, I would try. But there were too many stories never listened to, too many wrecked lives that had never been given a chance in the first place. I'd try – but there was only one of me, and so very, very many of these poor souls.

The first time I met Beth she came running towards me like a long-lost friend. She threw her arms around me and, as I extricated myself by moving her arms from my neck, it was like touching bubble wrap. Looking at her arms as she stood back, I could see there was barely an inch of space from her hands to her elbows that wasn't covered in scars of various ages. Old white-silver ones, recently healed pink ones and newer angry red and purple ones. Her fingers were various shapes and sizes. At first, I thought it might be the result of a medical condition, as it was unlike anything I had ever

seen. I was quickly inform
her repeatedly putting them
the door shut.

Beth was very outgoing on
smiley, chatty, pretty girl who ta
an hour. However, if you were d
when she wanted to speak to you,   you
were ignoring her, that mood would   in the blink
of an eye. She would walk away without a word and start
smashing her head into the nearest wall and would only
be satisfied when she could see blood on the paintwork.
She had initially been diagnosed with an emerging
personality disorder, an ambiguous term given to young
people who display antisocial behavioural traits along
with other mental health symptoms that can't be defined.
As she got older and more details of her past became
known, it changed to PTSD with severe psychosis.

When talking to people, she would discuss her
childhood as if it were idyllic. I wondered what had been
so traumatic in her past that it still affected her to such
an extent – I knew I wasn't getting the full story about
Beth. I'd heard people talk about her dad being in prison
but hadn't given it much thought. She could be quite
precocious when she wasn't the centre of attention and I
naively assumed that her mum may have overcompensated
by showering her with attention.

As time went on, one thing that working with people
like this taught me was never assume anything.

five years old when her reception class raised concerns about her behaviour. Her case stated that she felt her language was 'sexualised' and 'too mature' for her age. She referred to her chest as 'tits' and would try to entice the other children to put their hands in her pants. Social workers and educational psychologists got involved but found nothing of concern and decided that she was just advanced for her age and needed appropriate sex education.

When Beth was nine years old, a teacher again raised concerns that she appeared to have started her periods but had no self-awareness. She would walk around with blood running down her legs. After a meeting with her mum, Beth was given sanitary products that she kept with her at all times and was advised on how to use them.

At twelve she collapsed during a PE lesson that she wasn't participating in because of 'girls' troubles.' She had been sat on a bench at the side when she passed out. An ambulance was called – and subsequently so were police and social services. Beth had miscarried.

When interviewed with her mother present, Beth made several references to not wanting her dad to get in trouble. This in itself aroused suspicion and, after an investigation and search of their house, over 1,200 images of Beth were found. These horrific images of child abuse were all in the most serious category and many officers said they were the most distressing they had ever seen. They began at birth, and showed Beth's father and male acquaintances raping and inserting objects into her. Beth's mother claimed that any abuse must have taken place while she worked nights as a nursing assistant. This was doubted but never disproven and she was never charged with any offence. She came to visit Beth in the unit several times a week. Her father was sentenced to sixteen years in prison.

Beth received counselling but often wouldn't engage and, as she entered her teens, her mother could no longer keep the child safe as she would abscond, be sexually promiscuous, drink and self-harm. She had been sectioned after trying to drink bleach, severing the end of one of her fingers in a door and then trying to stab her mother all in the same day.

I've seen pictures of Beth when she was around ten or eleven, looking so innocent with perfectly smooth arms and legs. By the time I met her at fourteen, her arms and legs were a mass of scars and welts. She was unrecognisable.

Beth was very jealous of other girls and would be flirtatious with the male staff. This in itself I found to be a concern and raised the issue with the manager, who agreed and implemented a female-only policy with her. That arrangement went totally out of the window if Beth tried to hurt herself. She would ligature repeatedly and smash her head and face into walls and doors until she had to be held. She was a strong girl and, despite the female-only policy, male staff would inevitably be called upon to restrain her. If males were on her observations, checking on her every five minutes to ensure her safety, she would lie on her bed naked so that they would see her when they looked round the door. She saw herself as nothing more than a sexual object and she didn't know how to function without that kind of attention. It was all she had known.

Beth never discussed what had happened to her. In quieter and more lucid moments, she would rest her head on my shoulder and say that she wished I had been her mum. She was just an innocent teenage girl who had never experienced a childhood. She refused to discuss her experiences and it was thought to be too damaging to push the issue, so the only management of her trauma was by medication, much of which she would refuse to take or pretend to take and spit out. The only measure of her recovery and progress was by the number of incidents she had. This was all well and good but what next for children like Beth? She couldn't stay behind locked doors for ever and she wasn't being equipped with how to deal with the outside world and recover from the devastating events that had so far been her life.

I asked about this many times, with varying senior psychiatric consultants and doctors, and was told that the reality was she would probably spend most of her life in a secure unit as there wasn't any treatment out there that could help someone recover from the kind of trauma she had suffered. She had been written off already. Now eighteen, she is classed as an adult. I know that she lives in a form of secure supported housing for adults with mental health problems. I only hope that she proves everyone wrong and is able to salvage some happiness out of the life that she was dealt.

Lee and Beth gave me strength in their own ways – but I didn't realise how much until Ellie. Being with them, being with all the other Lees and Beths and Ellies, made me realise that I needed to take a stand, but I also knew that I had to wait for the right moment. Eventually, I knew, I would do it.

I would fight for myself.

I would fight for the women who are told they are nothing.

I would fight for the children who have no one.

I would fight for anyone who needed me on their side.

Too many people had tried to take all of that from me. Martin tried to make me nothing. He isn't alone. There are so many men out there who are just like him. Good husbands, pillars of the community, respectable citizens, adoring fathers. It's all a front. Behind closed doors, the mask drops and the bile (or the fist) rises. Martin never hit me, but when I was on the receiving end of that bile, I always felt that no one cared.

Now I wanted to take my resolve a step further. I wanted to be there for every woman who has been in my shoes, or who is still living that nightmare. I wanted them to know someone cares and it's not just words. I wanted to do something that would make a difference. I got out and I was ready to fight – to fight against everything Phil and Mother and Martin had done to me. I didn't want to feel shame any longer; I wanted to inspire. When I thought of how quickly Martin had started controlling me, I realised that I had been primed for him. That is also what had happened with Lee and Beth and so many other children in care or in the system. They were abused and defiled in so many ways before anyone stepped in – if they ever stepped in – and they were prime candidates for more abuse, just as I had been.

I wanted to do something – but, first, it seems I had to meet Ellie.

CHAPTER 16

Ellie

ELLIE'S MUM, SAM, first started to become concerned when, at three, her little girl still had difficulty talking.

Although Ellie was her first baby, Sam's intuition told her that something was wrong and that the little one wasn't progressing the way she should. After Ellie's fifth birthday, there was a dramatic change in her behaviour. She became aggressive, moody, violent and argumentative. Her mum became so concerned that she took her to the doctor and asked for a referral to CAMHS (Child and Adolescent Mental Health Services). CAMHS offered to give Ellie a course of Ritalin, often used to treat ADHD, and said that if it had no effect, then there was nothing wrong with her. They also advised Ellie's mum to go on a parenting course.

Once it was discovered that Sam had had no mother in her own life, they put Ellie's problems down to her parenting, justifying it by saying that she hadn't had a role model so therefore didn't know how to effectively parent the baby. This really struck home with me as it could so easily have been my life they were talking about. Knowing all of this wasn't true, Sam asked for a re-referral.

Apparently, this referral got lost in the system and Sam tried to deal with Ellie's growing problems by herself for years, unsure of how to deal with bureaucracy, unsure of herself. By the time Ellie was twelve she was very violent, and her behaviour was becoming more and more challenging. She frequently stated that she wanted to die. She hated to be touched, particularly by men, and would become fixated on certain things. Sam struggled to cope and keep her safe, and eventually returned to CAMHS and demanded a new assessment. This time, Ellie was diagnosed with Asperger's, a form of autism. After this diagnosis she was admitted to a psychiatric unit for two weeks, which she would go on to have constant nightmares about.

When Ellie was thirteen, with the situation untenable for both her and Sam, she was taken into respite care. Sam, by her own admission, couldn't cope any more. Ellie was continuously violent, battering her mum with hockey sticks, and displaying bizarre behaviour such as sleeping outside. She went to a care home for children with autism, where she was placed with four staff at all times. This lasted for only six months before they decided she was too dangerous to manage. From there Ellie was transferred to a home for children with emotional and behavioural problems.

Mixing with other kids who had complex problems, she began sniffing aerosols, jumping in front of cars when taken out, constantly running away, and other learned behaviours. She was put into inappropriate restraints, but after six weeks, social services and CAMHS again decided that she couldn't be safely managed. They took her home with the support of two carers, who would sit watching TV while Sam again tried to manage her. Ellie was, by this time, making frequent attempts at overdosing, but despite this she was allowed to walk out of her care home with a bag containing many weeks' worth of strong medication.

After a further assault on Sam, Ellie was arrested and again taken to respite. After several weeks they wanted her to go on home leave. Ellie had been speaking to Sam on the phone and had told her that if she managed to get out on leave then she was going to kill herself. Sam's warnings were ignored and hours after being allowed to go on leave, Ellie banged her head so hard that she needed a brain scan.

Between the ages of thirteen and seventeen Ellie was moved between nine different placements. Put on a vast amount of medication, while in care she had gone from weighing ten stone to twenty. At a leaving party at one of her placements, she ran away and jumped on a train to go home to her mum. Sam met her at the train station – but so did the police, who immediately tried to grab her. Despite Sam's warnings that Ellie didn't like to be touched, they went ahead. It took twenty-six police officers to restrain her. Ellie was arrested, stripped naked, placed in a paper suit and held for forty-eight hours. When she was released she had a black eye, a cut on her head and an eight-inch scar on her leg. She was also charged with six police assaults.

At court, with her autism recognised, a placement was ordered for her and, just before her fourteenth birthday, she was sent to a residential school for autistic children.

Ellie was there for a year. She was put on a range of antipsychotic medications that were designed to calm her down but, in reality, had the opposite effect, which can often happen with a mix of such drugs. Ellie told staff she felt 'wrong' and unwell, so they put her on a higher dose, which resulted in her being in a heightened state. Threatened with having intramuscular injections, she ran away and jumped in a river. She was brought back and often refused to come in at night, so they would often leave her to sleep outside. Finally the unit had to admit they were unable to meet her needs and she was transferred to a secure unit.

★ ★ ★

Ellie

Placing someone with autism in a secure unit is akin to putting a claustrophobic person in a confined space. They are highly sensitive to noise, so are faced with sensory overload. Along with the inconsistency of rules, staff and routine, it is completely inappropriate as it's the policy of these units not to accept anyone with autism or drug-induced psychosis. Despite this, patients with both are regularly admitted. The system is not just flawed: it is completely wrecked.

By now Ellie was fifteen. In a rare counselling session, she disclosed that she'd had 'sexual intercourse' at the age of five with the son of a family friend. This was reported to the police and Sam accompanied her to be interviewed. The police didn't question what Ellie meant by 'sexual intercourse' but Sam told them that her daughter had said the thirteen-year-old boy 'lay on top of her with his willy out' and that she had also been forced to perform oral sex. While it was still abuse, it wasn't intercourse – however, Ellie had spent ten years thinking that she'd had sex at the age of five, and it was no wonder she hated physical contact with males.

Sam was accused of helping her daughter too much in the interview and Ellie was scared into not taking things any further by being told that she would have to face the accused in court if she wanted to press charges. The issue was dropped.

Ellie was never going to be able to make progress in

the environment she was in. She was, effectively, set up to fail. When she continued to have 'incidents', it was decided that she should go to a medium secure unit. This was a stage up from where she had been, with only maximum secure being above it. The unit in question was a forensic unit, meaning that the people there were in the criminal justice system as well as the mental health system and, when Sam wouldn't consent to allowing Ellie to be placed somewhere where there could be sex offenders, the professionals decided the only option was for her to be discharged home again, with no school, no respite and no support in place.

Meeting after meeting took place to try to find another suitable placement for Ellie, but every option was dismissed as being unable to guarantee her safety. At a care and treatment review the CCG (Clinical Commissioning Group) demanded that social workers find a placement, but several months later Sam received a letter stating that, as she'd been unwilling to engage with services, they felt that she no longer needed any input from them.

The next day, Ellie was hospitalised for nine weeks. Following her discharge, she was allowed to sign her own Section 2 paperwork to have her mental health assessed. Not deemed to be in care or have learning difficulties, and now aged seventeen, she was placed in a house by herself with carers. All kinds of plans were made for her to enrol in the local college and do voluntary work at a charity shop – all things that were completely unrealistic. Ellie couldn't even have gone alone to the local shops, never mind attend a college with hundreds of people. Again, she was being set up to fail. The 'innovative' approach of trying to mainstream someone with complex needs also included allowing her to come off all her medication at once.

As Christmas approached Sam became more and more concerned that every time she spoke to Ellie, her daughter became easily upset. That wasn't Ellie. Laughing or angry, yes, but she was very rarely tearful. She was looking forward to Christmas though, and on a home visit on 25 November she watched the local lights getting switched on, decorated the tree with Sam and talked about her Christmas dinner. The next day Sam visited Ellie at the house to drop off her iPod that she had left behind. Unimpressed by the state of the house, Sam made a complaint. There was grime everywhere and no curtains up at the windows. It was completely bleak and she hated to think of her daughter there as Christmas approached.

The following day Ellie seemed particularly down. Concerned by both her low mood and loss of appetite, Sam felt that the lack of meds was causing a depression to get hold of Ellie. On 29 November, Ellie spoke to Sam on the phone and asked for headphones for Christmas. It was a normal conversation, but when Sam told Ellie that she was going to her sister's graduation at the weekend, Ellie wasn't happy and again became upset. Sam explained that no one else was going but Ellie put the phone down. She then called her gran and uncle to complain that she wasn't allowed to go to the graduation. This was entirely normal behaviour for Ellie; she would have a moan about something and obsess about it a bit until something else came along to occupy her mind. Sam knew that she'd just have to wait, and that Ellie would move on from her gripe.

It never happened.

The following afternoon, police came to Sam's door and delivered the news (in front of her young son) that Ellie was dead. She had ligatured with her own clothing while 'Killing Me Softly' played on her iPod. She had been upset, distressed and asking for help, but she was left alone for sixty-two minutes unchecked.

Fifteen minutes would have been too long to leave Ellie in that frame of mind, let alone an hour. She wouldn't have needed isolation, she would have needed someone to be with her until she felt better.

I knew none of this had happened until five months later. I was sitting relaxing with half an eye on the TV, a cup of tea in one hand and mobile in the other. I would usually go through my emails when I left work, but today, for some reason, I hadn't. I scrolled through the usual suspects – offers that must be seized before midnight, the latest fashion, film, book releases – hardly looking at them. I selected 'delete all', but then one of the email addresses caught my eye. I looked back at it and saw that it was from a former patient. She hadn't used her usual address, so I'd dismissed it initially. She was someone I'd worked very closely with and, after her being discharged and me leaving my previous job, we'd kept in touch. It was usually an update about how she was doing. After a big operation and getting back to work, I hadn't replied to her messages for a little while. But this email said: 'PLEASE READ!!!'

I clicked on it and read the brief few lines she had written.

I stared at the TV some more, then read it again. It may as well have been written in a foreign language for all the sense it was making.

It said that Ellie was dead. That she had killed herself last November. She wasn't sure if I knew.

NO, NO, NO – I DIDN'T know! It wasn't true, it couldn't be true. Patients cut off from the outside world often only get to hear fragments of information and can run with it. Before you know, it has grown legs and arms and tails. This is what was going on here, I was sure of it. I'd worked with hundreds of people who were mentally ill and suicidal, and you could have told me that any one of about half of them had killed themselves and I wouldn't have been surprised. But not Ellie. She was a little girl in a young adult's body. She lived from moment to moment and, because of her autism, most of her actions were born out of frustration at the world.

She had made suicide attempts throughout the time I had worked with her, but always when she knew someone would be able to see and stop her. She just needed people to understand how she was feeling in a way that she couldn't articulate. This wasn't true. I Googled her name, sure that it was just the rumour mill of adolescent girls, and her beautiful smiling face popped up. It was a photo of her with her arm around her little brother, whom she adored. She was wearing sunglasses and they were both smiling. It was a lovely photo, but it wasn't the photo I was seeing. It was the headline underneath, which read that tributes had been pouring in for a seventeen-year-old girl who had died suddenly.

I have lost people before; I lost my own sister too soon, but this felt like someone had kicked me in the stomach. I read every article I could find; they all showed Ellie's gorgeous face and said she had died suddenly, giving little or no other information. Maybe it wasn't true that she had killed herself. Partly because of her medication, Ellie was a big girl, so maybe she'd had a heart attack. It would be no easier to bear but it would have been unpreventable in many ways. Ellie *WOULDN'T* have deliberately taken her own life, I told myself. Frantic, I read and reread it. I didn't have a Facebook account, but I opened one just to try to contact Ellie's mum Sam to find out what had happened.

Sam and I had always got on well and she knew how

much I thought of her daughter. Working so closely with young people who are in such a dark place, you can't help but get attached and Ellie was lovable, funny, witty, bright. I adored her. Although very childlike, she had a way of seeing right through people that was beyond her years. Her laughter and smile could drag you from the darkest mood, and I wasn't ready to give up on her.

I managed to trace Ellie's uncle and sent him a very brief message asking if Sam could contact me. It was only five months after her death and I could barely imagine how she was coping, or if she would want to talk. I didn't want her to think I was being insensitive, but I also didn't want her to think I didn't care. How could I have not known? I thought about Ellie a lot but, in my mind, she was settled at home or in a suitable placement where she felt safe and people understood her little ways.

Her uncle passed on my contact details and Sam messaged me later that night with the full story.

Ellie's discharge from the hospital where I had cared for her hadn't been the happy ending I'd hoped it would be. She had ended up in a care home for young offenders. They knew she was autistic and needed things to be done in an ordered fashion. She had been in the bath and they asked her to get out to see her social worker. This isn't as simple as it sounds; Ellie needed to know what her day would consist of and who would be working with her. She would find any unexpected changes to her schedule very frustrating and distressing, as many people on the autistic spectrum do. She got out of the bath but was upset and distressed. Ellie asked if she could talk to someone and was told to go away and get dressed. They then left her with NO observations for a full sixty-two minutes.

Ellie was partially institutionalised. She was used to having staff with her constantly and being observed frequently. After she'd been left for an hour on her own, staff entered her bedroom with difficulty. She lay pressed behind the door. She had used her dressing gown belt as a ligature and, when that hadn't worked, she had removed her pyjama bottoms and used those too. It was something she had done many times before, knowing that staff would check on her any minute and intervene. On those occasions, she would get things off her chest and admit that she just wanted people to understand how upset she was. She was left for OVER AN HOUR. Knowing of her previous attempts, knowing she was upset, knowing she had asked to talk to someone.

No one had listened.

She would have expected someone to stop her.

They didn't. She really was gone. I wanted to swear, scream and punch someone and shake every person I came into contact with and say, 'Look what's happening, no one looks, no one listens – people will keep dying; young, innocent children whose only crime is to have suffered traumas that their brains don't know how to process.' These kids vent all their hatred on themselves. I know how their brains work because it's how I used to feel and how I still struggle not to feel half the time. It's why I left the field that I loved working in – because I couldn't keep watching the same failings, the same negligence, the same lack of care and provisions for people who had already been through so much. I wanted to make a difference and I was swimming against the tide. I withdrew into myself and cried constantly for weeks. It was all I thought about, and I couldn't take it in.

I had spent a year keeping Ellie safe. She had spent her life fighting to try to get well, only to be passed from pillar to post by people who were incapable of meeting her needs. I was sick of it. I was sick of people getting away with neglect and failure to provide a duty of care; with mistreating people under the guise of being 'professional'.

I'd had no one to speak up for me until I became strong enough to do it myself – most of the amazing people I worked with will never get that chance because they are labelled. No one wants to listen. If what they say is uncomfortable or holding someone to account, then it's put down to the ramblings of someone who is not in their right mind.

Yet people say, 'Why didn't they say anything?' The truth is, they DID. Each time they hurt themselves, each time they cried, each time they got a new scar they were begging to be asked, for someone to see the pain inside of them, but instead they were treated like naughty children. They are medicated to paper over the cracks of pain that inevitably seep through like damp through the wall. The core isn't treated, so it continues to grow and grow until the drugs no longer work and have to be changed and the cycle starts again.

Ellie's death did something to me – it triggered a need to inform people of what goes on in some of these institutions and secure units. There is a system that continually fails the most vulnerable people so catastrophically, and it is shielded behind government policy, bureaucracy, 'safeguarding' procedures and inspections.

I feel there was no place for Ellie. No place that could meet her needs, keep her safe and help her find her place in the world. Her story, and that of the others, is not unique. There are many more Ellies previously, presently and, sadly, no doubt in the future who will face the same obstacles. Mental illness is now at epidemic levels in the UK and the very places that are meant to heal and help people who have often had the most unimaginable experiences are failing in their duty of care. Children as young as twelve are left in secure units, miles away from their families, with their only human contact coming when they are restrained. Little wonder that many of them create incidents in order to gain that human contact, even in a negative form. Grown men are allowed to put teenage girls in painful holds but God forbid any female staff lend an ear to them or they will become 'too attached'. We can't lay a soothing hand on their back because that would be 'inappropriate' but young women who have been victims of abuse and rape can be grappled to the floor by men twice their size. There is a hidden secret world behind locked doors that needs to be exposed. Records are falsified, abuse takes place on a daily basis and children are deprived of their most basic needs. Investigations, such as the BBC *Panorama* programme's coverage of the Winterbourne View care home abuse case in Bristol, in 2012, have highlighted the issue but people need reminding that this was just one case where abuses were found out. How many go unnoticed or are not cared about?

What I have said here only skims the surface, but after I found out about Ellie, I felt I really needed to do something. My mind wouldn't stop; it was constantly racing, trying to process the flashbacks that flooded over me. It didn't matter if I was trying to block them, it didn't matter if I was trying to address them – they were just racing towards me, filling every sense I had.

Okay, I said to myself, to some other part of me. *Okay, come on. Do your worst – let me have everything.*

I sometimes think that survivors of abuse have learned to cope so well that no one really knows what it takes to function each day. We carry so much inside us, inside our heads and our hearts and our bodies, that it weighs down every happy thought, every little bit of joy we are allowed to experience. The weight of it is something that no one truly understands unless they have been through it. It is more than depression, it is more than anxiety, or PTSD; it is a boulder that we drag through every moment. Sometimes that boulder weighs less than other times, sometimes we can even forget it's there as the power of other positive things brings us a strength that allows the burden to feel lighter – but it's always there. That doesn't mean our abuse defines us; it just means that we have . . . *something*. The something that has been done, the something that we carry.

When I started to put together the parts of my life – what Phil had done, what Martin had done, what I had seen being done to those vulnerable children – I wonder whether there was part of me that thought, NO! No more. Take the easy path, shut up and just appreciate the life you now have.

I can't do that.

I feel I have a responsibility to these children in care, in our mental health services system, to let them know that someone is listening, and someone is shouting. And I have a responsibility to me. Although I wasn't born with learning difficulties or a condition like autism, I know their pain and I could so easily have become trapped in that system too. I have carried my past for so long, always terrified that I would be judged by what other people did to me, rather than for the person I am. I thought I would carry labels for ever, just as I thought I was marked as a child and young woman when Phil and Martin targeted me. I didn't want that, I wanted people to see past what had been done to me, but there was always fear – fear that I was broken, fear that I was damaged beyond repair, and that others would only see that.

Writing this book has been an incredible journey. It takes a lot to bare your soul, to put yourself out there to be judged, and it has been a rocky path. There have been times when I have thought that I wasn't abused enough to justify taking this step, that I wasn't damaged enough by it all. What I've realised, though, is that you never know when your words might touch someone, when they might offer hope or strength. Phil was found guilty. Should I really feel that my story would be more 'worthy' if he had done more to me and others than the appalling things he did do? I would never think like that in relation to someone else's experiences, and that is something I really want to emphasise to all survivors. Be gentle with yourself. Imagine that someone else is telling you all of these things that you have been through. Would you really speak to them the way you speak to yourself? I bet you wouldn't, I bet you would be kinder to a stranger than you are to yourself.

It's true that some mornings you wake up and wonder

if you can keep going – but you need to hold on to those other mornings when you wake up and know that you'll be fine. That you have been through so much, for so long, that you will navigate the bumps and troughs in the road, that you will find your own path and you will make your own way.

Looking back on it all has made so many things fall into place and has made me realise what matters in my world. My brother Andy has been my protector for so long. He gave me away at my wedding and has been the sort of man I could depend on for many years; but I wish that it hadn't been up to him, or any of my other siblings. I wish my mother had been able to love me. The fact that she always acted as if I was a burden has affected me; it has made me question whether I am worthless so many times in my life, and I fully believe that it led to me being abused by both my uncle and my first husband.

I had been primed for that role, the role of the girl or young woman who felt she had no worth. Abusers sense that, and they exploit it, and I was told from such an early age that I meant nothing, so why would I suddenly wake up one day and dispute that? It was as if my mother couldn't ever let any affection in to our relationship. The cursing at me, the constant references to me thinking I was better than anyone else, took their toll. 'Princess Kate,' she'd snarl, 'frigid little prude, aren't you?' I was a child. She should have done something, she should have acted on that quivering pervert sitting beside me, shoving himself close to my terrified little body, looking like he would combust if he sat there a moment longer. When he sat there with a coat over both our laps, why didn't she act the way she should have? She should have been a mother – even animals protect their young.

If she had, and I had been allowed to be a child, would that have made me less susceptible to Martin? I think it would. I had only ever been told that worth came from a man pursuing you, from wanting to have sex with you, and my boundaries were practically non-existent. I had grown up not knowing what was normal and what wasn't. I was too young to understand the world Mum had taken me to; I was too scared to shout any louder. I had no idea if other uncles did these things, if other uncles slept with other mums – I was just lost in the middle of it all.

I know now that opportunistic paedophiles, like Phil, convince themselves that the child wants it to happen. The way he stared at me was something that couldn't be avoided. I would eventually have to look at him, and that – in his perverted mind – meant that I was initiating the abuse, I wanted it and I was a willing partner. When his lawyer told the court that Phil was no danger because he had walked away from a toddler in a supermarket who was looking at him, a toddler who Phil believed was trying to initiate sex, that made some of the puzzle slot into place for me, as I realised he had actually convinced himself those things happened. He had told himself that children initiate sex, that they seek it out and that they are willing partners. What chance did I have against that sort of twisted logic?

CHAPTER 17

Ellie's Inquest

ELLIE'S INQUEST TOOK place over two days in October 2018 and was heard by HMC Mr Taylor at Preston Coroner's Court. Her mum Sam, her grandma, family friends and relatives and I were all present.

For two days we heard from various witnesses who had been involved in Ellie's care at various levels. We heard from a lovely doctor who had gone over and above in his duty of care in keeping Ellie with his service because he knew that if he discharged her from his involvement – as the rules said he should have done – there was no other place or person to pick up where he had left off. He also explained to the coroner that, despite many ligature attempts, Ellie was always apologetic afterwards and would admit that it was her frustration to feel 'normal inside her head' that made her do it rather than a real desire to die.

There were many contradictions in what was reported – for example, as reported by staff from the same company, Ellie's mood was stable on the day of her death, and also Ellie was in low mood on the day of her death.

When all of Ellie's challenging behaviours and self-harming history were being detailed, though, there were things that shone throughout, agreed on by everyone no matter what they had to say. Everyone was in agreement that Ellie was an extremely bright girl who needed extreme structure and routine in her life in order to make sense of the world. She requested staff rotas two weeks in advance so that she always knew ahead of time who she could expect to see on any given day. Given that everybody agreed this point, it seemed remarkable that it wasn't adhered to and that a social worker had visited Ellie unannounced, knowing how this would affect her.

The fact that Ellie, a girl who needed consistency, had so many different staff changes was always put down to 'structural team changes within the department'. The home that Ellie had been placed in was available rather than suitable. They clearly couldn't meet her needs and had admitted in an earlier multi-agency meeting that they were unable to guarantee her safety.

Everybody was also in agreement that when Ellie was about to self-harm or attempt a ligature, she only ever did it when she knew staff to be around and she knew people would intervene and keep her safe.

The main thing to come out of the inquest was that it was blatantly clear that there was nowhere suitable for Ellie to have been placed. In the absence of any newly built specialised units, this means there must be many other young people with needs as complex as Ellie's, those with mental health issues, emerging personality disorders and autistic spectrum disorders, who are experiencing the same failings.

It is apparent that when someone has multiple diagnoses, as Ellie did, there is a passing of the buck as to who should take responsibility for their care. With Ellie this was further exacerbated because of her age. As she was seventeen, Children's Services wanted to pass her to Adult Services but Adult Services deemed her to be too young. Autistic spectrum professionals felt that mental health professionals were best placed to support Ellie and mental health professionals thought that autistic spectrum professionals would be better at doing that. In the meantime, poor Ellie was moved from placement to placement with ever-changing staff and new faces, not knowing who she could trust or where she would be in the next few months. Is it any wonder she craved some continuity? All she could do was to put her trust in the staff who were assigned to her at any one time and believe they would keep her safe.

The statements given by her support workers state that

Ellie should have been checked every fifteen minutes when in low mood and every thirteen minutes when in a stable mood. Leaving aside the discrepancy in the reports about what mood she was in, she was left for sixty-two minutes without being seen or checked on, following an incident that they should have known would unsettle her: the unannounced social worker turning up when Ellie was in the bath.

In summing up, HMC Mr Taylor firstly offered his heartfelt condolences to Ellie's family (none of the people who had 'cared for' Ellie had even said 'Sorry for your loss' to Sam) and thanked them for all their input and questions that had enabled him to reach his conclusion. He referred to all of Ellie's many positive qualities, which Sam had mentioned in her brief statement in the court, and that the professionals had also alluded to, and said that this was the picture he wanted those who loved her to hold on to. He noted Ellie's many complex needs and praised the level of love and care she had received from her family.

The purpose of the coroner's court is not to apportion blame or liability and this point was highlighted to everyone present. The coroner's job is strictly limited to answering four questions: Who died? Where did they die? When did they die? How did they die? When considering this last – and hardest – question, Mr Taylor said he had to consider whether Ellie intended to take her own life or if there was an alternative explanation.

He referred to Ellie's histopathology report, which said that both methods of self-ligature that can be applied bring about unconsciousness extremely quickly with an extremely small window of opportunity for resuscitation. Finally, he said that there was insufficient evidence of definitive intention to end her life and as such he was recording a 'narrative verdict'. This option post-dates the old verdicts and is now referred to as a conclusion. A short form could have been given of 'suicide' or 'accidental death' but Mr Taylor chose a 'narrative' as he felt there was more to take into consideration.

His 'short form narrative' conclusion was as follows:

Ellie Jaye Sumner passed away on 30/11/2017 at Buckshaw House in Chorley. She had a history of self-harm and a diagnosis of autistic spectrum disorder. She died from tying a ligature around her neck in a locked room after not being seen or spoken to by staff for some time.

This ended the proceedings. There was a sense of many unanswered questions but relief and gratitude that the coroner had shown such empathy. Those two words at the end of his narrative conclusion said everything. Ellie had not been seen or spoken to by staff for 'some time'. 'Some time' was too long. Far too long for poor Ellie.

There was one trip we had to make before I left Sam to come to terms with the events of the day. Ellie's property was ready to collect from the police station. Just her mobile phone, nothing else. Sam signed for it and was handed a crackly plastic bag with the one item from her daughter's too-short life in there.

Just a phone.

Nothing else.

A phone with a pretty cover, a cover that Ellie had chosen.

I looked at it and my heart broke as I read the words embossed on it.

Never Grow Up.

Epilogue

I NEVER REALLY thought I'd get here. I didn't think I would survive the abuse, or the gaslighting, or the bulimia, or the self-hatred. Once I had my children, once I had those gorgeous, pure little souls in my world, I had something to hold on to – and that's what we all need. Make sure there is something else that you can love more than you love yourself, for when you think you aren't worth it, when you think the world would be a better place without you. You will get there with 'you', but, on the days you can't, turn to something or someone else.

I wish Ellie had known that she mattered. I wish other people had recognised what she needed and that they had worked a damn sight harder to keep her in this world. I want her story to be acknowledged, and I want everyone reading this who has felt lost to know that survival is hard, but it's worth it.

Survivors need to learn how to love and how to trust – and they need to know that they themselves need love too. You might have to learn it all over again, or you might have to learn it for the first time, because there is no doubt that the skewed experiences of some childhoods make it a daunting task.

I wish I could hold Ellie now. I wish I could tell her that, just because your wings are broken, it doesn't mean you won't be able to fly one day. She will never know what she has given me, that the heartbreaking waste of her life has inspired me to finally find my voice. For years, everyone told me to be quiet, to never say a word, to never answer back. In the end, without the unacknowledged strength of that shattered girl, I would never have got here.

I want my life to be filled with good things now. I want to start looking for the sunshine instead of the dark clouds. I want to dance and love and hope, because I know that life is too short and there are too many people who want nothing more than to crush your spirit. Move away from them, move away from whatever keeps you in that place where you were a poor, frightened child.

You can make your own ending, you can write your own script. You will never know how happy you can be until you try. For me, my happiness lies in my children. That doesn't mean that I put pressure on them to be everything for me, but it does mean that I acknowledge and adore just how much they mean to me. I would relive every harrowing moment of my life a million times over if it meant still being left with the four amazing babies I have. They are all so different, yet so similar in many ways: they have been the light in the darkness throughout my life. They made me want to carry on when I felt like giving up, keep me striving for a better life, and to be a better person. They are my reason for everything and the reason I am now strong enough to tell my story and stand up for things I believe in.

As I come to the end of my story – *this* part of my story, as I'm sure I'm not done yet – I want to take a few moments to talk to each of these wonderful people who I made, and who, in turn, have made me who I am.

Katy – my brown-eyed girl: to me, you are still my sassy little playmate in a princess dress holding on to my leg. You have a soft side that not too many people see, and I couldn't be prouder of the beautiful, independent, confident, ambitious, loving, caring, amazing woman you have become. You're still sassy and I know you will never allow anyone to silence you about things that matter. You are my best friend, always spurring me on when I feel low, always there with a hug that only you can give. There aren't enough words to express how much I love you, how much I have always loved you since the moment you burst into my life twenty-eight years ago (and hijacked my birthday!). I love you baby girl.

Joe – my floppy-haired boy. So quiet, always thinking

way too much and feeling things so deeply. You don't wear your emotions on your sleeve and I'm privileged to be one of the few people who you will openly share your emotions and affection with. Handsome, intelligent and articulate, you are one of the most loyal people I know, a person who will take secrets to the grave with him. Forever a friend to me when I need it. I am so proud of you. Always striving to be the best, you don't realise that you already are. I love you more than life.

Alex – my dimples. What a journey we have been on. Always only mine; we were inseparable for the longest time. I look in your gorgeous face and still see that cheeky little boy who has always made me smile every day, and continues to do so. You have overcome so much and my heart bursts with pride to see the amazing man you are and what you are achieving in life. Clever, funny, loving and caring with such a strong sense of family and that contagious laugh. My world would be dark without you in it. My love for you is unconditional and everlasting. I love you, dimply boy.

Oliver – our bear. My baby and the baby of the family, what a boy you are. With a head older than your years, always so sensible and mature, you have never caused me a moment's worry. Your heart is huge, always thinking of others and with a constant supply of cuddles, and I feel so lucky to have you. You are as beautiful on the inside as you are on the surface, and I know you will achieve all your dreams, my gorgeous boy. I love you all the world.

Epilogue

These are the babies I made, and the babies who made me. Whatever I went through will never impact on the purity of love I feel for them and, to me, they are a symbol of the fact that I *can* get things right. All of us survivors have those moments (or days or weeks or months or lives) when we think, *Ah, but I deserved it; I didn't say 'no', I didn't shout loud enough, I wasn't smart enough to stop him or stop what was going on.* And that voice, that negativity, is very strong, very powerful. To have something, someone, you can look at and see as wonderful, as deserving of love, cannot be argued with. There are times when I talk to myself terribly, say horrible things, but I would never stand for anyone criticising my children. I allow myself a tiny bit of pride that I made them – that those wonderful people came out of me.

I have been told to stay quiet for so long, to not say a word, to put up and shut up. Whether I was being demeaned and blamed by Mother, or abused by Phil; whether I was suffering years of gaslighting by Martin or being told that I needed to just close my eyes and my mouth to what was going on with vulnerable children, I have always been told that my voice should not be heard. I have had enough.

I won't be quiet any longer.

There is nothing I can do to change what happened to me as a child, or as a young woman, but I can set the course for the rest of my life. Yes, there will be dark times. Yes, there will be days when I wonder if I have done the right thing. Yes, there will be nights when I can't sleep for the anxiety and the panic, as the blood pounds through my veins and I wonder if I am strong enough to do this, to shout for me and to shout for others.

Yes, there will be all of that.

But, I will hold on to the fact that I have now taken all of what happened and looked at it face on. It doesn't scare me any longer, because I survived every last bit of it. In fact, it lights a fire in me, it lights a fire that will help others, the children who are still ignored, the young people who are locked up and abandoned, whose pasts are dismissed and whose futures are written off. Everything in my own past has brought me to this point, to the stage where I know that I want to use all of those injustices to scream from the rooftops that we are failing children every second of every day. We are throwing them on the scrapheap after they have been broken by others, shrugging our shoulders and saying *nothing can be done* when EVERYTHING can be done if we have the courage to fight for it.

I don't really want sympathy for what happened to me, what was done to me – I want understanding. I want people to understand what it means when they ask, 'Why didn't you say something?' Every individual who thinks the victims are responsible because they never spoke out needs to look at where they are laying blame. There are no shades of grey with child abuse, no subtle nuances. If you are not supporting survivors, you are excusing perpetrators.

Acknowledgements

I WOULD LIKE to thank my dad, brothers and sisters for the happy, innocent first eight years of my life that no one can take away from me – I love you all so much and that little girl will always be a part of who I am.

Thank you to Katy, Joe, Alex, Paul and Oliver (in the order they entered my life!) for endlessly believing in me, picking me up when things looked hopeless and always encouraging me to pursue my dreams and try to do things I thought were beyond me.

A huge thank you to the lovely Ciara Lloyd at John Blake Publishing for believing in my story and continuing to shine a light on the tales that other people want to ignore. I very much hope I will get the opportunity to work with you in the future, Ciara, as you have given me such a great opportunity here.

The same thanks go to everyone at John Blake Publishing for making this book and others like this possible and giving people like me closure and the chance to help others.

Thank you to Kerri for picking up Ciara's mantle in her absence (for the best baby-based reasons!).

Thank you to everyone involved in the case who stepped forward and turned their own lives upside down to speak up and stand by my side. It is not for me to mention names, but you know who you are. It will never be forgotten, and I hope that you too get the closure you deserve.

Thank you to Greater Manchester Police and my liaison officer for dealing with my case with such compassion and dedication.

And finally . . . Linda-Hyphen-Brown, as I like to call her. One of the loveliest, most caring, talented and genuine people I have ever met (though she will hate me saying so!). Thank you doesn't seem enough, but I'll say it anyway – thank you for your patience, for your generosity, for being someone I trust without question, and for your dedication to getting my story heard. There is no one else I could have done it with.

If you would like to get in touch with me, please email on contact@kmauthor.co.uk and I'll endeavour to get back to you as soon as possible.

Acknowledgements

**In memory of
Ellie Jaye Sumner**